Dumped!

*A single mother
shoots from the hip*

Caroline Oulton

✳ **SHORT BOOKS**

First published in 2006 by
Short Books
3A Exmouth House
Pine Street
London
EC1R OJH

10 9 8 7 6 5 4 3 2 1

A CIP catalogue record for this book
is available from the British Library.

Cover illustration and those on pp 25, 153 and 187 by Kate Sheppard

ISBN 1-904977-28 6
(978-1-904977-28-5)

Printed in Great Britain by
William Clowes Ltd, Beccles, Suffolk

JACKET DESIGN: NICK CASTLE

Contents

Introduction

The Road to Recovery

However sleek and well serviced a vehicle you were, zooming down the highway of your life before that crash, you may now feel that you have turned into a dilapidated, not to say dangerously erratic, old banger overnight.
You may feel that you will never be able to move again. But don't worry – here is your... ROUTE MAP!

And finally...

Dos and don'ts to keep you on track

A thrillingly uncharted landscape as well as a million other possible journeys await you. Go girl!

For the lonely millionaire who sought out a confused and majorly up-the-duff mother of two for fun and fireworks. Time to roar. Time to soar. Thanks for everything Mr Moore!

Introduction

This is a book about what to do, how to cope, and how possibly to protect yourself from total meltdown when your partner and the father of your child or children dumps you and bloody well trades you in for someone supposedly 'better'. Better as in younger, prettier, warmer, cooler, less tired or more understanding? you wonder wearily to yourself. I assure you that his flawless new floozette might be any or all of these things; but in the end his gruesome switch in allegiance is likely to come down to one sole factor — his new lover is novel and with all the motivation in the world you cannot reinvent yourself in that way and therefore cannot compete.

So, when you have been dumped – and God knows it is grim as absolute blazes for ages and ages – this book might with any luck give you a bit of a boost. As you peel yourself off the kitchen floor, dust yourself down, and try miserably to reassemble your identity, you deserve repeated reassurances that what has happened is not all your fault and does not signal the end of a happy family life.

All the rules you used to live by seem to have changed overnight. How do you keep your cool and preserve your sense of self in this uncharted mucky morass?

It is hellishly difficult and you might resort to doing or shouting things that in the past would have been unthinkable, even abhorrent to you, just to stop yourself from going under. How you cope does depend to some degree on your temperament and if I suggest or admit to things that you personally find repulsive or unacceptable I do apologise.

With hindsight, I have reluctantly to concede that, as the wronged woman, I did become an irrational termagant overnight, a violent, overbearing, quarrelsome blusterer who squinted out at the world 24/7, as they say, through a hideously distorting green mist of tear-ful hysteria.

Inching away from the horror of that particular phase does feel like an impossibly fraught journey a lot of the time, but you will eventually make it through – you will arrive intact at what sometimes seems to be that ever-receding goal, a calm and stable existence and, with a bit of luck, eventually join the growing gang of empowered, effective, cool and content single mums.

What this is and isn't...

This is not a manual for single parents in general, nor is it a book for single dads. They have their own problems, God knows, and I could not possibly comment. Nor does it include chapters about how best to nego-tiate bad marriages, infidelities, trial separations, or both parties agreeing that sadly they seem to have 'grown apart'.

It does not include sections packed with the phone numbers and web sites of professional arbi-trators or family lawyers either, although there is of course a need and a place for all of that information. Neither is it a book about putting your children's needs ahead of your own, or about trying to understand how you yourself contributed to the break-up of the relationship. No no no!

This book is emphatically and unashamedly aimed at and written for women, married or not, who were in relationships to which they felt committed, with a child or children, and who have been left against their will by their male partners. Partners who have elected, usually in rather a sudden and brutal fashion, to live with – actually, principally to shag – someone else.

It is designed as a map, a possible way forward, but also aims to be a consoling lucky dip and pot pourri of anecdotes and advice to sample along the way. I hope it might ease that very particular dumped mum anguish even slightly, and occasionally help you replenish your dwindling resources. Above all, though, I want to convince you that you are not entirely alone and that all is not lost with regard to your future happiness.

❋ ❋ ❋

Sometimes being a dumped single mum can feel as though you have inadvertently joined a new all-female club. You do not really understand the point of it, or the rules, but you totally identify with all the other members. When I was traded in for a younger woman and left holding two devastated small children, I needed shed-loads of support. I needed advice and affirmation of myself as someone that did still exist and was not irredeemably boring, unattractive and generally crap. I needed dos and don'ts and I found that I got them generously and unconditionally from other women, some of whom were in the same boat and some of whom were about to be.

It did, though, take me an absurdly long time fully to accept that I was not to blame for what had happened and that there was no major stigma, embarrassment or inherent tragedy built into being a single mum. In fact, as I eventually discovered, there were a lot of us out there in almost identical circumstances. We all had kids, had all been dumped by our exes and there was actually enormous solace to be had from swapping traumas and toddlers and wine and indulging in endless circular conversations that began and ended with 'That bastard!' It was one of the few things in those bleak early days that really helped.

And that morale-boosting support is exactly what I aim to convey in this book, in the hope that it might help you to cope a bit more quickly than I did with the emotional hurricane currently upending you, as well as signpost a few of the lurking abysses you are liable to tumble into along the way.

Your anguish will continue for a long time, as will that peculiarly impotent despair of witnessing your kids' loss, but you do get through it somehow. You do; you will; you can. And, after a while, you may to your amazed disbelief notice the occasional upside to your new solo life.

A bit of background...

I met my partner when we were both twenty. After initial infidelities and false starts, we stayed together for just over sixteen years – pretty happily in so far as these things can be judged. Twelve years in, we had a son followed by another one two years later to the day. Even though we never married, that mutually agreed process of having children together did constitute – for me anyway – the most binding 'contract' with another adult I could ever imagine.

But then, when the second child was about a year old, my partner, who, for convenience's sake, I shall now designate 'The Bolter', 'got very close to' a colleague whom he had 'admired' for some time. Initially, I was convinced that somehow we would be able to get through the affair and out the other side. But, after a desperate year of trying to sit it out and much corrosion of my sense of myself, not to mention the wake-up trauma of one particular row which descended into the first and only time my partner actually hit me, I told him that if he would not agree to stop seeing 'her' then he had to move out.

He was clearly desperate to leave; he just hadn't wanted the guilt of taking the decision himself. Yet years later he was still intermittently claiming that I had been responsible for the split-up since I had asked him to go. (What I had failed to realise was that it had suited him to hang on and time his departure to coincide with a working stint abroad as that way he could sidestep much of the messy emotional fall-out.)

After a short hiatus, he duly set off abroad with his wife-to-be and her little girl. Any communication we managed during our first year apart was poisonous and fraught. He dangled the possibility of returning, said he had contemplated suicide, but was adamant that, yes, he was still madly in love with his new partner.

My sons were utterly inconsolable. They cried through the nights, wet their beds constantly, were miserable at nursery, did not want to eat anything and then cried themselves to sleep again each evening. The three of us zombied through those first few months somehow in an exhausted and desperate haze.

A number of well-meaning people told me categorically that it would take me about two years to get over the split. That, as I found to my cost, was far from the case. More realistic for me was another rule of thumb: that it can easily take you half the time again that you were together to negotiate your pain down to even remotely bearable levels.

Now at last, more than ten years in, I can say with truth and certainty that we could not, and should not, get back together. It may seem odd to register that in this context, but I was never of the I-never-want-him-near-me-again school of thought and action. On the contrary, my jealousy, pain and plummeting self-esteem were all so acute, and the spectacle of my children's uncomprehending agony so distressing, that, for literally years – yes honestly, and my horrified onlooker mates can testify to this – the only bearable end I could envisage to this wretched shambles was his return to our household. I was unable to conceive of any other way to repair the wreckage that he had left in his testosterone-fuelled wake.

I wanted my boys' father to live with them, I didn't want for them ever to have to live with some other adult who was no blood relation of theirs, be it a new partner for me or a new wife for him. I categorically refused to think of myself as a single parent since that suggested an irrevocable change and I feared it would confer on me a permanent sad, victim status. I also hated it when people, understandably enough, described us as having 'separated'. I wanted to scream at them, '*I have not separated from him. I haven't gone anywhere...!*'

Slowly, slowly, though, in this new, partner-less, domestic configuration, I started to readjust, to make plans, and even occasionally to look cautiously ahead into the future. Little by little, I began to heal up and to relish taking decisions and making arrangements and, most significantly, to enjoy the children's achievements by myself. I could and did share some of those special child-learning – to-ride-a-bike-type –moments with grandparents, aunts, uncles and, occasionally, even with my ex. But crucially, life no longer seemed utterly futile in the absence of him in the way that it had when he had first bailed out.

Simultaneously, his own exciting, new, till-death-us-do-part-not marriage was starting to crumble. The kids and I rarely got inklings of the subsidence, as he never discussed the state of his relationship, not even when said wife and stepdaughter finally moved out of his life for good. By then, though, I had finally realised what my family and friends had known emphatically for some time: *there was no going back.*

Since 'it' happened, I have talked to a fair number of women who have gone through the same thing, experiencing almost identical despair, and a wholesale, long-term loss of confidence. Our exes, albeit different in many ways, employed such astonishingly similar excuses — largely, we suspected, to help themselves negotiate their own guilt — that we were at least able to console ourselves with the banal predictability of male behaviour.

It may be much too early in your own traumas even to acknowledge the possibility of any joy or sunshine in your daily existence ever again. I promise you that I lived in a relentlessly dark place for what seemed like an unconscionably long time. Now, though, this minute even, I feel excited to be surging through life with my kids pretty much unaided and almost wholly unimpaired.

So here's how...

Blizzards and black ice

Some of the hazards to watch out for in those difficult early days.

Loneliness

Loneliness can creep up on you, stalk you and cripple you without your even realising that it is lurking in the vicinity. I may sound like a talking poster on the wall of a doctor's waiting room but it is true. I was so pole-axed by despair, the kids' despair which was even more unbearable to try to deal with than my own, not to mention trying to hold down a pretty scary job even though I felt so comprehensively crap

I almost could not drag myself out of bed when the mornings finally came, after wide awake nights of blackest despair, that I did not, guess what, notice in addition that I was also incredibly lonely.

I suppose – as I could no more have gone out in the evening than flown to the moon – if I had thought about it or even recognised the loneliness chewing away at me, I would not have imagined that there was a solution anyway. I did not feel in any state to cope with company.

You feel so defensive and somehow inept that you have let this happen to your family that you cannot bear to face people. It is such a comprehensive and public humiliation I think, and for the first few months you feel so protective of yourself and the kids that it is impossibly difficult to bare your misery to the world, to admit to yourself, let alone anyone else, that you might be lonely.

In those early weeks you are much more likely to curl up, withdraw, protect yourself and try, understandably enough, simply to limp from day to day, putting one foot in front of the other, vaguely attending to your kids' basic needs and occasionally remembering to wash your hair or face.

In my own case I alternated between being a

slumped heap and a demented dervish:

I wanted money from him, no I bloody didn't. He had to see the kids this instant. How dare he presume to think he could visit his sons? I wanted to see him: no I SO didn't. I wanted to look gorgeous; no, I wanted to look ravaged, destroyed and betrayed. I wanted him to think I was happy; no, I mean, I hoped he would think I was suicidal which I was pretty much, well, not really, of course, because of the kids, and so on and so on...

All this was desperately tiring and there seemed to be nothing I could do to moderate the erratically contradictory urges coursing through my veins like some weird drug. Try to remember that early on you are in a turbulent and unfamiliar place with your needs and emotions yo-yoing about all over the place. Your perspective on what seems to be happening to you shifts violently and unpredictably several hundred times a day. It is unwise to take too many public stands or irrevocable decisions at this stage.

Here is one small example. My kids missed their father so horribly that one day I found myself looking at a big solid chair in the kitchen and wondering if I could conceivably designate it as some kind of father substitute that they could climb onto and into when their pain was especially acute. Fortunately, a friend made it clear that this was not a useful notion and I still flinch at that particular memory of my post-dumped nuttiness, supremely grateful that I had been dissuaded from telling my already confused children that chairs could easily be dads!

Things will be further confused in the immediate aftermath by the fact that each time you feel something or think you do anyway, you do so much more emphatically than usual. I REALLY hated his guts. I REALLY wanted to kill her. I would have hit anyone who suggested that I was volatile or inconsistent but with hindsight I know that I was totally off the scale most of the time on most fronts. One close friend reminded me of this recently and I still feel anxious about the number of people I subjected to that madly see-sawing persona.

Remember also that you will almost certainly be deluded about how well you are actually coping. You may not realise quite how grimly haggard you have become.

Months and months in, my sons' nursery school teacher said to me heartily:

'That's the first proper smile I've had from you in six months.'

'I have been smiling,' I snapped back defensively

'*Those weren't smiles, they were grimaces,*' she retorted.

Another mate cautioned me not to fade away.

'*I haven't lost weight,*' I snarled, wondering simultaneously why all my clothes had stretched and I felt permanently cold and shivery.

These kinds of reactions are not surprising. It is unhinging to be in the grip of such strong and contradictory emotions. It is exhausting and scary and the only help I can really offer, with no definite time frame I am afraid, is to advise you to dig in, hold on and wait till the horizon has stopped tilting about like a crazed spirit level. Remind yourself that you are in shock and that in the circumstances it is not remotely pathetic or abnormal to feel sick all the time and be unable to sleep or eat properly.

Try and stay calm. Take deep breaths. Keep that handbrake on, as it were. Get drunk only with people you like and trust, snuggle up like a wounded animal under several hundred duvets and do not make any major social or physical demands on yourself for a good couple of months. Do not worry about anything inessential and if people offer to help out in any way, spoil you, cook meals or whatever, for God's sake put your pride firmly on the back burner for the moment and let them. You are having a foul time and you do not have to be supermum, superwoman and supercool as well. You really do not. Above all, do not beat yourself up about not being able to glue your family back together again. You can't and it's not your fault!

But beware. After a while, if you fail to address it, loneliness can stymie you, send you off course, stop you getting better and making progress. Even if the thought of company appals you in the early days, do try not to let yourself get too isolated. Undemanding mates popping by with their kids, or trips to the park with sympathetic neighbours will distract you and the kids, and possibly give you some respite from your non-stop despair however short-lived. Force yourself to sob your way through a bottle of wine with a nice friend at your kitchen table now and again.

I only actually realised how unbelievably lonely I seemed to have become when our funky nanny split up with her lover and moved into our basement. As I pottered around, sorting out makeshift furniture for her, I realised to my surprise how much I welcomed the idea of another adult in the house.

I discovered as I cried myself to sleep at night that I was gladdened by the sounds below me of someone else in the bathroom, or the front door banging as she came in late. It soothed me and I felt fractionally less abandoned.

Fortunately, for me this girl was great to live with, sympathetic, witty and wrestling with the trauma of her own break-up. In that respect I was lucky and, when she moved on to teach, even though I could not have conceived of anyone more sensitive to share my post-traumatic split-up emotional disorder with, I found that I was fine on my own.

Different people have different needs, but once I was through the initial startling loneliness I actively cherished being the only adult in the house with my growing kids. I love my relationship with them and I love the fact that, once they are catered for, I do not have anyone else to worry about.

My evenings these days seem luxurious and self-centred. I can get in the bath for hours, read books or the papers or trashy magazines, watch videos, have a girlfriend round and generally recharge my batteries for the professional and domestic assault of the following day.

There is still the odd twinge of loneliness, but these days I recognise it and deal with it. It no longer seems like a monstrous stalker liable to wrestle me to the floor in a big sea of misery, which it did, largely unrecognised, in those days immediately post-dumpage.

Do not expect to outwit loneliness altogether. You are undergoing a massive trauma and change of routine as well as everything else. And sometimes it will find a way of creeping up on you again. Whatever the lifelong regrets, though, that savage, biting 'aloneness' does not last when there are boisterous kids growing up around you – that much at least I can promise you.

The Other Woman

To her friends and family the Other Woman is no doubt charming, warm-hearted, loyal and generous; but the jilted partner, abandoned on the hard shoulder, sees things very differently. This Other Woman appears to be a flipping hazard – indeed she can turn out to be one of the major obstacles between you and any sort of attempt at forward motion. She is slippery black ice, treachery and danger personified.

I do not think any sort of journey can begin without addressing this socking great obstacle that is in your way. You need to get past her somehow. So let us try and boot her into the rough as an absolute priority.

May I kick-start the process with a few useful definitions?

Doxy… A beggar's trull…

Trull?

Concubine,

A drab, strumpet, trollop, wench…

A lewd woman… belonging to the lower orders: common, vulgar, unskilful, wicked, unprincipled, ill-conditioned, good-for-nothing, worthless… poor, sorry, lascivious, unchaste…'

Yes I think we get the picture. Where to stop? Where to start? I am not remotely proud of this but I used regularly to fantasise about killing her, my Other Woman, as it were. There. That is as good a starting point as any, is it not? These fantasies must somehow have seeped into my children's unconscious as fairly soon after being dumped, I got a call at work asking me to come and remove my troubled son from nursery. He was demanding a bomb so that he could blow up his father's new girlfriend!

These admissions and observations are not for the resolutely generous or faint-hearted among you. It may be different for you but in my mind the Other Woman had become a toxin that needed repeatedly to be purged from my system by screaming and yelling about her perceived shortcomings to anyone who would listen. She was stuck in my soul, in my life, and in my actual path for much too long.

A sympathetic shrink, with whom I had three sessions paid for by work, told me that this notion of mine was misguided. He told me categorically that my belief that, if I screamed about the fact of her enough I would eventually vent all the poison that I was projecting around and about and onto the notion of her, was incorrect. Jealous emotional bile he claimed did not work like that, and could not be dealt with in this way. He was a professional and may well have been right in theory and on paper but what did he really know? I wondered tetchily. There were dear little Barbie wellington boots lined up neatly in his hallway and warm baking smells wafting unhelpfully under his consulting room door during our sessions. How could he begin to understand how it felt to be a dumped single mum? I had to do *something*, and vilifying her was one of my pitifully few options.

In my defence, I can say with absolute certainty that my assorted dumped friends needed to discuss, analyse, rant about and despise the Other Woman just as much as I did. We could no more have ceased and desisted in that particular pastime than greeted these

Other Women civilly in the street. But, as I say, we are all different and, if you are one of those who has no quarrel with the woman your partner dumped you for, then please do fast-forward through this next bit.

Everyone, close friends and families included, reminded me with monotonous regularity that my ex was actually the culprit and that he should shoulder at least an equal weight of my wrath. I was still in love with him, though, and with my warped logic felt that, if she had never been born, I would not be in this particular and apocalyptically unbearable mess.

I was unhealthily interested in every last detail I could possibly glean about her habits and appearance. I needed to find out everything I could about her and it was a bad illness for a long time, as everything I discovered just made me feel worse. Her good points in that, yes, she was of course thinner and younger than me and knew more about his work, made me feel worse. The bad things – and, yes, in my version at least, they filled several telephone directories – made me feel equally bad. Why had the man I loved chosen someone with such apparently glaring faults over *me*? It was a lose-lose scenario, my fact-finding, but I just could not stop.

Various well-wishers and bystanders advised me

to leave it alone and stop speculating about the pair of them, but that was about as helpful as telling me to stop breathing. I needed to know, was *desperate* to know in fact, what the pair of them were doing, eating, laughing about and generally enjoying together. Then, when the odd stray fact did find its way back to me via the children or friends, I felt even more demented as it was never enough, never satisfying, never the whole picture.

You know that you are regressing right back to the playground by indulging in this sort of behaviour. When the boys told me she could not go out in the sun without being slathered in mega sun-block I even exulted in this revelation as a sign of her inherent weakness.

How wet, how sad, I thought, my ex certainly won't want to hang around inside with her all summer!

You read signs that are not there convincing yourself that he is unhappy, or that she resents your children and is about to leave him, whatever, *whatever...*

In reality nothing that you find out changes things, or makes any of it in any way better, but a lot of us find that we cannot help ourselves. Jealousy is a demoniacally possessive emotion and, God knows, one does not enjoy being made almost insane by it. It contaminates us and it is not as though we can just turn it off like a tap. Many of us would prefer to be graciously generous in sexual defeat I imagine, but we are only human.

I remember The Bolter saying pityingly to me once:

'Your anger is all about sexual jealousy isn't it?'

To which I screamed back:

'And what's wrong with that?'

I think by that I meant that, as I still loved him, then surely it was normal to feel jealous. If I still felt connected to him, then sexual jealousy was neither surprising nor inappropriate. It was hardly as though we had had an open relationship.

The situation is not helped by the certain knowledge, deep down, that there is actually a lot to be jealous about. How can sex with someone you lived with and have had kids with conceivably compete on the same terms with new, guilty sex with someone you have only recently undressed for the first time? I know that it cannot. Men find new sex pretty exciting and often confuse it with love. It is quite similar in some ways. There is that unattractive maxim, after all:

What do men need?

Food, shelter, pussy and strange pussy.

You probably had great sex when you got together, and then you had kids as well, which is quite intimate as links go. You may think that I am digressing here, but I am not. The kid or kids that you had are proof that you did it. That may seem obvious to everyone, but it is not a fact that always fits altogether happily into your ex's newly rewritten, post-your-life-together history.

'We were more like brother and sister really.'

Oh yes? Did you shag your sister and have kids with her recently? Hello?

So they, him and her that is, have suddenly discovered mind-blowingly satisfactory mutual emission of bodily fluids and are daring to patronise you with the hot news that 'it'/'love'/'sex'/'lust' is of more importance and significance CURRENTLY, than anything else. Yup. The trouble is that ninety per cent of your ex's staggeringly swift shift of loyalty here is down to sex with someone new. And that is why it is almost impossible to be cool about the Other Woman.

I remember The Bolter being extremely shifty around the whole subject of sex with his new amour, mumbling that that was not what it was about and anyway he was not actually living with her yet and, shuffle, mutter, change of subject. I think he wanted to convince me as well as himself that the whole deal was much bigger and more cosmically significant than just that little ole sex thang!!

Shortly after he had left, I remember, a swanky invitation arrived in the post addressed to them both. I saw it on the doormat and felt dizzy and nearly threw up. They were together and I knew that they were together but I really was almost explosively affected by the invasive fact of her name linked with his. I suppose that a lot of the time, in those early days, I had to kid myself that she did not really exist simply in order to get up in the morning, but that kind of hard physical evidence was impossible to dismiss.

Equally hard to dismiss were the lovebites on The Bolter's neck revealed in all their unglory one day by a new and ill-judged haircut. Ironically, at the exact moment I realised what they were, as in not the bubonic plague, my ex was in the middle of lecturing me about my own apparent loss of dignity. For months afterwards whenever he came to pick up the kids, a ghostly image of her dangling vampire-like from his neck appeared to me each time he strode up our garden path.

When my son told me that his stepmother had helped him to tie his school tie when he had stayed there, I had to exercise almost superhuman restraint not to burn the tie instantly or at least boil-wash it in superstrong bleach. The knowledge that she had touched something that my son wore was unendurable. Any reminder of such domestic proximity can enter your bloodstream instantly and then play havoc with you for days. One thing that I really could not cope with was the particular smell of the conditioner that seemed to yell at me exultantly that The Bolter's shirts, her undies and my son's dear little Mickey Mouse pyjamas had all been spinning around together merrily in their doubtless state-of-the-art washing machine.

You try not to think about her but you cannot help it. You pretend that she does not exist but she does. How do you get past this? How do you get past her? Should you meet her? This is one of the billion-dollar questions you may be faced with. I would say on balance almost certainly *not*, unless you are a superhumanly calm, controlled and deeply poised human being. Of course one has periods of wanting to meet them, to tell them what they have done to your kids and your life… but in the end there is no point. They are usually in denial about all of that anyway.

That said, the not-having-met-her can drive you quite demented. You imagine intermittently that seeing her or confronting her might conceivably be of help to you in some way, but the truth is that, even if she does not overtly patronise you, you will still feel patronised because you both know that he has chosen her over you. If *you* had left *him* and then he had found someone, or if your splitting up had been mutual, it would obviously be a whole different ball game, but in the circumstances that we are discussing here, how in God's name can you be remotely civil if you glimpsed her while handing over your precious traumatised babes to your ex? Search me.

Some dumped mums, who have my everlasting sympathy, find themselves in the grotesque position of having regularly to be in the same room as, breathe the same air as, the Other Woman, and that must absolutely be nightmare central squared. A friend of mine's young daughter was in the same class as the Other Woman's son, so for ever afterward my mate would be subjected to this snooty, callous cow queueing behind her at parent's evening, sitting in the row in front at school plays and so on... And all the while, one presumes, shuddering – history didn't relate – the disgusting dad was – what exactly...? – commuting between the two women taking an interest in his daughter's brilliance in English and then doubling back to discuss his stepson's bullying and behavioural problems. Yuck!

In fact, you do sometimes hear stories of group Christmases or summer holidays where the two sort-of families join up. I remember one dumped mum regaling me with the horror of such a scenario which her youngish son had talked her in to, convinced it would be festive to have both parents and new step-mother together over Christmas; and the dumped mum could only afford very cheap presents and was given absurdly lavish offerings by her ex-husband's new wife, and had to sleep on a leaky lilo in the kitchen as it was a holiday house and there weren't enough bedrooms and everyone went sailing all the time and she was violently seasick and it was all quite scarringly hideous.

In what is rather a juvenile fashion, I know, even now and, although I am told that The Bolter and his ex-wife do not even acknowledge each other if they pass on the street, I still dislike her with an intensity that I know to be both outdated and inappropriate. She was certainly a catalyst, but these days surely she should be pretty much irrelevant to me. The problem is partly that at the time she was such a potent lightning conductor for my shame, jealousy and disappointment that I don't think I will ever manage totally to expunge her from my unconscious. Does it matter in the end if you continue to blame and loathe the other woman forever more? In one sense, I think, yes, it does. She is taking up emotional space that you need for other, more important things: your kids, your career, your friends, the good things that remain.

At some point, somehow, you have to exorcise the worst of your demons even if, when you are in the thick of your misery, it seems quite impossibly unrealistic.

Now I can safely say that, when some of my closest friends (well the still-married ones at least) made me feel unbalanced to the point of being a pariah for repeatedly vocalising my loathing of her and urged me to be positive and focus on her good points, they probably had my well-being at heart. I think for me that, although I was fabulously jealous of her, and the thought of her physical relationship with him did undoubtedly make me feel nauseous and inadequate and crap for ages, it was their whole *domestic set-up* that somehow hurt more.

It was the imagined jokes, nicknames, cinema dates, walks in the park that seemed more intimate and more of an unbearable long-term betrayal of me and us. The unbidden mental flash of them holding hands or watching late-night news on telly or going to a café for breakfast would take me by surprise and knock me badly off course for hours. I still remember my despair when one of my children asked his father on the phone what his wife was doing at that moment and he replied that she was cooking some rice. That simple fact preoccupied me for days.

And then, of course, there's the effect all this ranting misery has on the children. My intemperate and incessantly vocalised loathing of her was not the best thing in the world for my kids to witness but it was probably a damned sight better than their being exposed to an ongoing hysterical loathing of their dad. And where is all that pain and misery and jealousy and sorrow and loss supposed to go?

We read in endless articles that children often blame themselves for their parents' break-up and believe that if only they had known it might happen they could perhaps have prevented it in some way. This is awful and mortifying and, of course, never true. The fact is that children do sometimes need a sort of license to carry on loving *both* parents, and if one of them is a pitiful heap, periodically exploding with rage about the other, it is very difficult for them not to feel guilty about their continued adoration of the apparently injuring party.

In retrospect, I was probably too vocal about my feelings with regard to the Other Woman but my children were never for one instant allowed to imagine that *they* could have prevented their father going if they had been nicer or behaved better.

Denial

Denial is a more insidious hazard than the Other Woman but it can quietly mist up your windscreen and also make it more difficult for you to move forward. Early on, as I suggested, you might need to deny stuff in order to breathe – her, the fact that they had sex while he was still living with you, the fact that he lied to you repeatedly for months and months. Initially this is legitimate and sensible, otherwise the sheer scale of the accident and all its endless and horrific ramifications can quite literally floor you. You may also find yourself denying, again with good reason, the fact of his really having left for good. Time and again you hear supposedly concerned onlookers clucking:

'*Well, of course, she's in denial about it all, poor thing...*'

And, frankly, to some degree you have to be. The only way to tiptoe away from the emotional multiple pile-up you're currently inhabiting is to deny what has recently happened, or bits of it at least, as the gruesome new reality slowly starts to bite home. So, denial is a coping mechanism and is normal and fine, but you should eventually start to taper it off or you can risk becoming deluded, demented and out of touch with reality. If, five years after the split, you are still screeching to all and sundry:

'*I do not believe that this is happening to me,*'
then you should possibly start to think about getting a grip on the realities of your situation or, failing that, seeking some professional help.

I was almost certainly in denial for longer than was wise or healthy. Since I felt totally stuck in my misery and didn't know how to go forward, I thought the only option must be to go back. You hear of dumped mums who cling on to the hope that he will return, while everyone and everything else, including their children, are slowly starting to adjust to the new order. Nothing is to be thrown away or changed in any way, these mums in denial insist, and then, of course, on the rare occasions that the philanderer returns, those clothes don't fit anymore anyway. Denial can be a way of trying to freeze time, and life, kids and pain can't really be mothballed. It just doesn't work like that.

I know a dumped mum who has kept her season ticket so she can sit next to her ex and watch football with him once a week. Cosy or deluded? It can be a fine line.

Thank God, when I was badly stuck in an absolute swamp of pretending things were not happening to me that clearly were, my older sister somehow sensed the fact that I was in denial about a number of things and decided to intervene. She had been dumped a few years earlier and was therefore further down the road toward recognition of her reality than me. Finally, one evening she lost patience with talking to my bottom as my head was shoved so far down into the sand and yelled down the phone at me:

'Listen to me! He has left. He has married someone else. He is not coming back to live with you ever but being a single mum does not mean you have to wear a nasty brown coat for the rest of your life!'

I was shocked to the core and felt as though someone had thrown a bucket of cold water over me.

My sister was both merciless and adamant that the unwanted status of single-mummishness was not relentlessly ugly, threadbare and purgatorial and the end of the world for ever more. It was not something I could hide from and pretend was not for me and did not suit me for ever and ever. And she was absolutely right.

Perhaps my not slamming the phone down on her immediately marked the first little chink in the protective iced-over denial that was preventing me from seeing out, and clocking the road ahead. Time perhaps to squirt on some anti-freeze and let real life back in bit by bit.

Alcohol

Unfortunately, alcohol also comes into the black ice category, creeping up on you unexpectedly and sending you spinning out of control and way off course. It may seem a bit melodramatic to give over a special section to alcohol but it really can turn into your foe in these circumstances. Therefore, sadly, I can't just let it bob about hearteningly in the treats section as I would like!

A few shaky weeks after being dumped I was required to work in another city on a Sunday and my ex-partner came over to look after the kids. After an early start, a demanding day and a difficult train journey I felt horribly daunted at the prospect of coming home and taking over so that he could swan off back to his exciting new life! My best friend lived between the station and my house so I dropped by briefly to rally myself en route. She, single and theatrical, mixed a killer jug of cocktail to give me a boost. I had not eaten all day.

When I finally weaved my way home I was definitely less twitchily apprehensive than I would have been without the drink. On being confronted, however, at that late hour by children who had neither been fed nor bathed, a switch in my brain, which should have stayed down or half down at least, flipped straight up in one easy motion – activated by the alcohol coursing through my body – and I totally lost it. I remember feeling in that instant red-hot with anger and resentment. I screamed, I yelled and, as he fled, I rained objects down on him in the street out of the top-floor window, including some manky slippers that he had neglected to take with him in his initial sweep. It was a disgraceful display. I shocked him, which did not matter much, totally unhinged the kids, which of course did, startled the neighbours with details I would rather I had not broadcast in quite such an abandoned fashion, and squandered lots of ammo ineffectually. Not good.

A few years later I was at a private view and was introduced to a funny, self-deprecating woman who I immediately took to. She, it turned out, was a recently dumped single mum and, as we sniggered and swapped anecdotes and drank and drank, she got louder and wilder and the other people there started to eye us pityingly. I was less drunk than her and could see what everyone was thinking but at the same time I had total sympathy for her as I was her, had been her and knew I might well be her again if I was not very careful.

It is hard being a single mum and the end of the day can sometimes seem especially grim. There are whiney, tired children to give supper to and bathe, the washing up, the dirty washing basket that is out of control again, and no other adult around to roll your eyes at, or hand a child or a dirty saucepan to, cook you something or regale you with grown-up conversation. Even when the flipping clothes are clean and dry they still need to be sorted out and put away and the toys are all over the floor mocking you. And all of this with no apparent support, apart from mother's little helper in the form of that wicked new corkscrew you were given for Christmas. With one flick of those stainless steel levers you are in.

Sometimes, and especially in those unspeakable early days, I think a legitimate response most evenings is: fuck it. And why not? The trouble is that in my case it soon started to be every evening, and then it became a bit earlier and then the bottle of wine was not stretching to three or four evenings any more. I was feeling a bit crap in the mornings and looking a bit crap and when people rang after nine in the evening I was not entirely confident that I was not slurring and I realised that I had to get a bit of a grip. I did not stop drinking exactly, but I definitely slowed down.

It is hard to dish out definitive advice on the alcohol front as a lot of it is in the timing. If it helps, in the immediate aftermath, go for it, because you need whatever props and anaesthetic you can lay your hands on. Early on at least, you do have a bit of social license but as the months pass, beware the tongue-loosening, aggression, rambling phone behaviour and morning rattiness that will start to induce disapproval in even your closest supporters.

Remember that you are trying to alleviate loneliness and move forward *in a straight line*.

Revenge

This is the last in the major obstacles section. It is a lurking tarry mess that you may get stuck in for a bit but negotiating your way through and past it will mark the moment that you start to get seriously proactive in your journey outta here!

Hearteningly, my dictionary does not say that revenge is a misguided or ill-judged act. It is simply the doing of hurt or harm to another in return for wrong or injury suffered. Payback, in other words, or retaliation. Why then does revenge have such a bad press?

Over the years I have given quite a bit of thought to the subject of revenge. The widely held view that by indulging in any type or form of revenge you are 'letting yourself down' seems pretty unfair to me. Why should you be a patient Griseylde and not grizzle? All's fair, they say, in love and war. Well, he is in love and you are at war.

I was utterly unable to behave according to that well-nigh universal expectation that us hurt punished mums ought simply to button our lips, pick up the pieces and get on with it. To me it appeared that in the end the dumper's cruelty always seemed to be accepted by the world, in the interests of everyone getting on with life. That apparent indifference by society is hard enough for us dumpees to cope with, without having permanently to turn the other cheek as well. Why are women not allowed to register their pain and hit back, yes, even in little petty ways? Their men are expressing their feelings after all. And how. They are translating their feelings into seismic actions with unpleasantly destructive consequences particularly for their kids, so why are women immediately criticised for being sad, undignified and embarrassing if they lash out in turn? Eh? Let us face it, the whole godawful situation is way beyond the category of embarrassment before you even start contemplating any small acts of revenge.

Even so... revenge is a difficult call. I have been both the wronged, hysterically jealous woman planning impractically cataclysmic acts of revenge and then, slightly further down the line, found myself watching with concern women raving, plotting, and spiralling themselves into temporary madness as they in turn gear up for some form of retaliation. I think with the calmness of hindsight one can sometimes get it a little bit wrong. The problem with that old adage, (the one about revenge being a dish best served cold or whatever the hell it is) is that by the time it or you are cool then you do not care anymore and do not want to spraypaint his suits or chop his Porsche up into tiny pieces anyway.

One dumped local woman I know used to keep the muckiest of her baby's nappies to flatten under the windscreen wipers of the expensive new sports car parked provocatively by her partner outside his new girlfriend's flat. That seemed to me to be quite an eloquent and legitimate way of reminding her ex of the mess he had left behind him.

No, you cannot help feeling inflamed with rage and acting accordingly. But you can take simple precautions, so that, as you slowly haul yourself out of that revengeoid pit of despair, you are not overly mortified by memories of your past behaviour. Avoid, where possible, involving other people in your acts of revenge, *particularly* your children.

There are always double standards flying around, some of them brandished at you by your ex to deter you from acts of revenge. Once men have been exposed with regard to their own major transgression (viz. sex with someone else followed by removal of their physical selves from the familial home), they seem to want everything instantly normalised to include this new order of things. They expect all other pre-existing etiquettes, codes of behaviour and social niceties to remain intact. We often seem to be asked, by our frosty exes:

'*How on earth could you say/do/think that? What about your dignity? You're letting yourself down, you know, you really are. Everyone's very worried about you.*'

Not surprisingly men want the uglier consequences of their actions suppressed or at least kept tastefully out of sight. Well, tough. That is not always possible. Why should you continue to humour him, protect him with regard to his legitimate insecurities once he has so ostentatiously betrayed you? In those early days I was permanently exploding with high-octane self-pity and rage over the godawful, unendurable unfairness of it all. (I remember thinking the expression that your blood boils was biochemically pretty accurate.)

There are, of course, taboo areas even within the happiest of functioning partnerships and for the vengeful dumpee these can quickly become a deliriously tempting assault zone. Then again, perhaps 'revenge' is rather a strong word here... when all we are talking about is your realisation that your unwanted freedom means you no longer have to exercise restraint with regard to your views on his obsequiousness to his boss, his personal hygiene, or whatever the hell else.

These issues have always bugged you and frankly there is no reason why you should deem them off limits now. It's amazing how quickly they spring back into focus at the precise instant when he has changed his access arrangements at short notice for the fourth weekend running.

I also found that there was the odd exception to the 'try not to involve bystanders' rule. When my son was about to start his new school, I sent the headmaster a fairly dispassionate account of the recent upheaval in our family life. I explained that the boy's father, who had been the prime carer, had left home very suddenly to live with another family, that he had only visited his children once in almost a year away and this unsurprisingly had impacted on his son, causing some problems, which I then enumerated.

I wrote this letter to some degree to explain my son's behaviour, and the school claimed it had been helpful. It was also, of course, to afford me the gratification of sending a copy to my ex. He was livid, wanted it retracted; he did not under any circumstances want to be introduced to the school as a parent in that way, and so on and so forth. He had brushed aside my previous attempts to tell him how his son was reacting, suspecting me of exaggerating. But now, as this letter was for a third person with whom he wished to be in contact over his son, he was forced to engage with some of the uglier consequences of his actions and he did not like it one bit. The letter detailed accurately what had happened but it was also for me, a satisfying moment, I suppose, of revenge.

My sons could not read at the time that their father left, so I vented some of my misery via signs in the kitchen with quotes from the children about their sadness and some of my own replies and thoughts:

Q: *Has Daddy got a willie?*

A: *Yes, my darling that's the one thing we can be absolutely sure that he has got at the moment.*

Q: *Why does Daddy like her more than us?*

A: *I'm afraid that's something you'll have to ask him when you next see him etc, etc.*

Every time he visited, The Bolter would rip these placards down in a shouty rage, even though it was my kitchen and the boys could not yet read. He could easily blank out my sobbed anecdotes, it seems, concerning his sons' misery by slamming the phone down, but having it up on the wall in black and white for all to witness he found unendurable. As a form of revenge it did the trick anyway: by ripping down those notes he did at least reassure me that something of the

emotional havoc he was wreaking on us was register-
ing with him.

And that's the point, surely. One wants and needs
the satisfaction of knowing that the act of revenge,
one's little arrowhead, has found its mark. They have
hurt you and you want to hurt them back, to make you
feel better, to make them focus on what it feels like to
be hurt, and so on.

This must be pretty normal as an impulse in
extremis and I cannot see why we should squander our
desperately needed emotional energy in suppressing
our rage and bile, simply so as not to let the side
down.

Of course, some of this revenge will be directed at
her. If, as is very often the case, you wish neither to see
her nor speak to her, except of course in your wildest
and often drink-fuelled late-night fantasies, you can
perhaps still rile her at a distance. With a bit of ingenu-
ity, you should be able to get a sense of her routine,
and sweetly achieve disruption under the guise of your
children's welfare:

'No, I'm sorry I do need him back at that time as he's got
the dentist...'

'...Oh sorry, did you say you were going away that
weekend? I did promise him he could go to Daniel's party and

he's chosen the present and everything.'

Do beware, though, that these strategies don't slosh sideways disruptively onto the children.

I do still remember with a frisson of pleasure the various small ways in which I tried to put her out — just a bit. Since I was working, it did not matter to me which day my ex collected his children from nursery. So one day when I discovered by accident that his wife needed him to pick up her daughter from school, I stipulated that he had to pick up our boys on that day and that day only, claiming it was the nanny's evening class.

Why? Because it made me feel better to try and make things a little bit difficult for him logistically when they were permanently fraught for me. The truth is that I was sickened at the thought of his skipping home with someone else's child when he was not around to do that for his own kids.

Most men are crap with dates and I think on the revenge front it can sometimes be legitimate to compound the logistical traumas by playing them at their own game.

'But I'm sure I gave it to you/told you/e-mailed that they had that then... and this on that day... and, no, it can't be changed, I'm afraid. You didn't realise? Oh sorry...

you'll just have to change your plans...We agreed the kids'
social arrangements should come first wherever possible,
didn't we?'

There are, of course, and I come back to this again and again, the most stunning double standards at play, particularly in those hard early days. Men rarely have any sense of the additional pain they occasion in you by the bloody 'we' factor.

'Sorry they're back a bit late. We had a lovely picnic,
and Anthea thought they'd enjoy bla so we took them to...'

So, it is worth, even if you have no intention of being in a relationship yourself, giving a little bit of 'we' back. And I guarantee that he will not like it. No Sireee. It will be:

'Who/where/what/when/why did you let him give my
kids that computer game?'

to which the answers are, of course:

'Oh, I thought you'd met him, he's one of my work
colleagues — tall guy, dark... No? Anyway, he's been great
with the kids...'

So there we are. Little acts of revenge are usually legitimate in my book; just be careful not to let feelings of vengefulness take you over. This must be a short-term strategy to get you through the worst. For ages I obsessively conjured up serious ways to hurt him back or fantasise about how best to annoy her. Now, thank heavens, I do not. And you, too, must leave this stage behind and resume your forward journey.

Drizzle and road bumps

After the first major hazards, some insidious smaller obstacles to send you skidding.

Access

I had barely got those first major hazards behind me and gained a bit of confidence when I was almost knocked into the verge again. What really began to get to me were the endless traumas of having to negotiate my ex's access to the children, which at first, I must admit, felt more like theft — the nicking back of chunks of my precious family life and my sons' hard-fought-for and precarious equilibrium.

You do need to be vigilant here. Issues of access will almost certainly erupt onto the agenda before you can even bear the thought, let alone the reality of it. Cocksure lover boy will stride back over the brow of the hill to reclaim the children from their desolate, disorientated, dumped mum in her deep dark valley of despair before she has even had a chance to wipe her eyes and think what arrangements might suit her. Access can easily become a semi-official way of getting to you, at you, round you, and speedily normalising the whole shambles for him.

It is a tricky area, booby-trapped to the hilt with emotional and legal heffalump traps, often with a lot at stake for the single mum. One of the problems, I think, is that access and maintenance are supposed to be viewed separately but inevitably get unhelpfully commingled. Everyone has different views on the rights and wrongs of it all. My one bit of advice is that you should try and do everything in your power to avoid a court settlement as that can result in the worst possible scenarios for all of you, including the children, and be hugely expensive. To my amazement, different lawyers in the same firm totally disagreed as to which way a judge might have ruled in my case, although thankfully it never got to that stage. I remember, even so, feeling sick with waves of irrational fear that somehow if I did not stay permanently alert I might lose my children to their father and stepmother for months and months at a time. This is a common fear, whatever the individual circumstances.

Whether the man who has dumped you is disorganised or a control freak, you really are not under any obligation to commit to things months in advance. You might still be freaked out and unsure about your own needs, so be on your mettle! Obviously he needs time to settle into his new life, and yes, he will see his children, of course, and these weekends here seem to fit in with squash games and everything else he wants to do, so sign on the dotted line please and we can all move forward with little or no unpleasantness. Hello?

It cannot be fair. The whole situation is lopsided and hurtful and unfair from the off, and he should acknowledge that, and do all he can to compensate. Of course, he will not view things quite that way. But this does not mean that you should get pushed about too much. It is hard to resist the pushing, it really is, particularly as your ex thinks his new partner is great and wants to please her and therefore needs you and the kids to fall in instantly with his suggestions.

However lousy, lost and tearful you are feeling,

take deep breaths and dig in.

'*You're blissfully happy, and we're incredibly unhappy so don't you think you should try to accommodate us a bit more?*'

He is unlikely to agree, but it is hard to argue with as a position. The trouble is that us women are somehow hard-wired to be accommodating and helpful and to find solutions, usually by putting ourselves out. I had nightmare visions of myself dropping the boys off all the time at their father's new abode as he did not drive, or faxing him idiot-proof maps of where they needed picking up from, and so on and so forth. And I fought against these helpful instincts tooth and nail as I decided it was no longer his privilege to have that kind of support. I really did not want to extend myself still further by according him back-up that was a hangover from a previous, different and mutually supportive contract between us. I resolved that I would try to communicate clearly with him over the children's needs but that I would no longer help him out with the logistics.

It took me a while to refine this position as I felt oddly guilty about the whole subject of my obligations over his access to the children. I had no experience of how to behave and was angry, obstructive and placatory all at once. In retrospect that seems absurd as he had skipped off abroad with his new family, making access very little of an issue for the first year anyway. Indeed, in some ways, to begin with, I was urging him to come and see the boys rather than trying to keep him at arm's length. I think somehow that he imagined he was still significantly in touch with us as he got very shirty on the phone from America when I referred to his sons' need physically to see him. Is there really that much difference for very small children, I wondered, between being rejected or being put on hold as they see it, indefinitely?

A couple of months after he had finally returned, I was obliged to attend a two-day weekend conference for my job in Scotland. It was crucial for me to have rock-solid childcare in place, but the children's father refused to commit to doing it 'for me' even though he had no other plans. He said that his access to his children should not simply be to suit me; it should be designed to suit both of us. To which, of course, I replied that it had not suited me particularly well having sole care and responsibility for two upset and confused children non-stop for almost a year while he had been away working.

It later emerged that I had been pretty uncooperative as he saw it anyway when he'd first returned full of the joys of spring and keen to have access to his children at times that were convenient for him. And it was because of this that he was refusing to commit in advance to helping me out over the conference. That refusal irrevocably hardened my position. I quickly realised that access could not possibly suit both of us all of the time and that I could never afford to depend on him. Does this ring bells with other dumped mums? A hideous cacophony I bet.

So, rule number one: if you want to control the access situation in the early stages, try where possible to avoid putting yourself in a position where he knows you really need him to have the children. He can then threaten to let you down, which is immensely stressful, before upping his own demands as a result.

Clearly this is not always the case and good luck to the sane couples who can work it all out sensitively; but, in my experience, you, the dumped single mum, are almost always the one left holding the baby.

Do not be hard on yourself initially if you find it all very difficult. When your children first go to stay with him, try to find things to do that you can look forward to and might actually distract you from the absence, not to say gaping hole, of no sticky fingers grabbing at you while you shop or try to read a magazine. It is a bitter irony that the peace and tranquillity that you have fantasised about so often is now elusive because you are in such a bruised state, and you cannot seem to STOP dementing about what they're all up to without you.

When I first handed over the kids I felt as though elastoplast was being ripped off me, exposing raw open wounds which stung all the time that they were away. I disliked the nakedness of being by myself. I was not used to it, especially at night and found it a nasty manifestation of my singleton status. Faced with two empty bunk beds at midnight I could not delude myself that 'it' had not happened. I could not have imagined that I would miss the messy shambles of breakfast but I did. I could not settle to anything useful or gratifying. I could not use the time sensibly. I wanted them back.

I did try to pack out those bleak empty deserts with little treats that I could not easily enjoy when I had the kids with me. Once I even went to two films back to back. For a very long time, though, whatever lengths I went to, I still felt miserable and aimless. I defy anyone just to give themselves a talking to, flick a switch and party away instantly when the kids first stay over with him. This new and different misery and loneliness go with the territory. You may have been desperate for a break or for some help with the children, but not like this, and certainly not with her as their new companion. No bloody way.

I once overheard a man complaining to a mate in a pub about how stupidly unreasonable his ex-wife was if he returned the kids slightly later than the allotted time on a Sunday evening:

'She complains how hard her life is, and then she complains if I have them a bit longer and she gets more time off!'

I wanted to tap him on the shoulder and explain that I utterly understood her apparently contrary position. You would kill for a breather but it needs to be on your terms to be restorative, not just as an unsettling result of his sloppiness at getting the kids back later than agreed. When that happens it is anxious-making and not restful at all, as deep deep down there is always that paranoia lurking that he may have taken them to Australia on a whim.

There is also the thorny question of the Other Woman in their lives – how soon should it be before the children meet her if they have not already, and in what circumstances? It is not easy. If you suspect and to be honest, burningly hope, even if you do not want him back, that this new relationship is doomed, why should your kids instantly be catapulted into a dubious game of happy new families? This is of course what your ex probably craves and is determined to achieve to prove that he has made the right decision and every-thing is going to be totally super-duper fine pretty much instantly and all of that rubbish.

I remember my children coming home after one of The Bolter's birthdays in the new configuration. They had been encouraged to sing 'For he's a jolly good fellow', a ditty with which for good reason perhaps they were not familiar. That for me epitomised what I found so painful about 'access'. Rituals that had been significant for us as a family were now being hijacked and soured by this weird new order of things.

Some anxiety around access can occasionally be dismantled by a bit of forward planning. If there is a weekend, say, with an important family do that you really want the kids around for, warn him well in advance, ideally in an e-mail, so that it does not all unravel in poisonous recriminations nearer the day when he thought it was his weekend. I do absolutely know, though, that this is easier said than done, not least if there is something special HE wants to do with the children that weekend as well.

I got so demented with The Bolter's casualness with regard to future arrangements – even his committing to collecting the kids from school a couple of days ahead seemed problematic – that for a while I tried to get him to sign a diary as confirmation that we had had the conversation but even that did not work. He would sign, and I would still get a call at work from understandably impatient teachers that sobbing kids hadn't been collected again. That is horribly difficult stuff to negotiate with equanimity and the written proof that it was him that got it wrong was not ultimately very comforting.

Often your ex's new partner will make apparently non-negotiable demands on him with regard to the social life they now share. At the same time, don't ask me why, it seems that the dumping men become incapable almost overnight of assuming proper responsibility for their abandoned children. When you live together and a child needs collecting and another child is ill and needs to stay in bed, one of you will go and one of you will stay. Simple. But that situation, in his mind anyway, no longer obtains once he no longer lives with you, so what the hell are you supposed to do? Take an ill child out in a blizzard? Expect a five-year-old to walk home by himself in the dark, or yet again ask a favour of a friend or neighbour as your ex now has other more pressing domestic and social obligations? He will want access when it suits him and not when it does not. This is what I mean by the single mum often being left holding the baby, and therefore being due commensurately more control when it comes to stipulations regarding access.

Recently a mum I know was reluctant to commit her son to a Friday sleep-over with us as it was her son's weekend with his dad who had him on alternate weekends. In the event said mum rang me back in tears saying that the boy might as well come to us, as it was the third alternate Friday in a row that her ex had hired a babysitter to look after his son while he went out partying! You often hear similarly woeful stories of divorced dads sending cabs to collect children from parties, or whatever, as they are suddenly playing an immovable game of cricket with work colleagues even though it is the only weekend they can manage with their child that month. That refusal to prioritise the children seems to happen less with mums, in my experience anyway.

When The Bolter pushed and pushed for his very young children to stay the night on a regular basis in his new house with his new family, I resisted like blazes for all sorts of reasons. I couldn't bear never to have them on Saturdays, but at the same time a weekday night seemed unnecessarily disruptive and difficult to organise, until finally a friend of mine suggested that he have them on Sunday nights. This actually worked out pretty well from my point of view and I hope was better for the children than some other solutions might have been.

I worked longish hours, and weekday mornings, in spite of my best efforts, tended to be fraught as I battled to get us all lunchboxed and out of the house without porridge in our hair. As a result I was loathe to relinquish any of my lovely slopping-about-with-lashings-of-toast cuddlesome Saturday and Sunday mornings with my boys. It has to be admitted, however, that by Sunday afternoon I was often feeling a bit ragged and tetchy. The Bolter, on the other hand, when he scooped them up was bursting with plans and gave them lots of attention. Also for me, just occasionally, having a relaxed Monday morning rather than the frantic beginning of week kerfufflefest that we normally experienced was a pleasant novelty. It may not suit everyone, but as an eccentric solution to a difficult situation I proffer it.

Another problem which I do dement about endlessly with fellow single mums is the fact of dads being crap over so many of those all important child-related details. We have all lost count of the number of times a reading book went missing during an access sleepover, or their dad forgot to get them to school early for a performance assembly, or a key piece of kit was sopping wet. How can you relax when you know that, even though you have bought and wrapped an appropriate birthday present, sorted out the themed fancy dress, photocopied the A to Z and stapled it to the party invite with a dayglow circle round the address, as well as telling your ex repeatedly that he is giving another child a lift home, there is bound, despite every belt and brace in the world, to be some filthy dad-centred lash-up when you are in the cinema with a mate with your phone turned off. This will, of course, impact embarrassingly on you and the kids but will be absolute water off a duck's back to him. I guarantee Madelaine's mum's extreme irritation will not even register with him. Yes, I know this is a problem with live-in dads as well, but it is infinitely more difficult and unpleasant to negotiate when you are separated.

And then there are all the other seemingly tiny things, which can send you into a spin of paranoia and fury… When your kids have been staying with their dad and his girlfriend, for example, you may find your-self needing to know what they saw fit to offer your beloved babes for breakfast. Was it healthy, sustaining, treatish? At the same time you can't bear to be privy to that information and feel contaminated by even caring about knowing and demeaned by pumping the kids for bad dad data!

People, by which I mean close friends, regularly accused me of being unreasonable over access but there was something about the visceral physicality of it all, my beautiful children in his new house and car which I found quite impossibly hard to be calm about. I also loathed the insidious way that once my boys were over there on a fairly regular basis the detail of my ex's new life started to seep back into our household over and beyond the actual visits. I wanted our life to stay hermetically sealed from his and I fiercely resented the exchanging of items via the children between the two households. Once you're involved in access visits that is clearly unfair to the children and no longer possible to maintain as a position.

I remember when the boys made biscuits at his house they would proudly bring them back in empty herbal teabag boxes and offer me some. Years later I still feel like barfing if anyone mentions camomile tea.

My sons also returned from access visits with cardboard models they'd been helped to construct of their father's new house with crayoned-on carpet. Can you imagine? My kids would be inordinately proud of these constructions and would inquire anxiously as to their whereabouts for months afterwards. Somehow I could never quite confess to having binned them in a hysterical dawn rage at the inappropriately tasteless symbolism of having my ex's new residence recreated within his recent family home in this way. Now that many years have passed and his partner has moved out I do find it easier to contemplate their staying over with him.

I cannot imagine ever being wholly 'don't care-ish' about it, though, if I am being totally honest. There will always be – lurking deep down in my psyche somewhere – a faint residual competitiveness about whether they have had a completely brilliant time there.

Let me close on a heartfelt acknowledgment that maintaining your equilibrium, nay sanity, around the whole area of access is tough as bloody blazes and, if occasionally you feel that you are totally losing control of it, or yourself, you are screamingly normal.

Money

Money is defined as anything serving the same purposes as coin, which could, I suppose, be taken to include holiday homes, cars, pensions and all of that stuff.

Dividing your income and assets when you split up is impossibly complicated, with endless variables: who worked, who gave up what to raise the kids, who inherited money, who squandered money, who needs what to live on, who is greedy, who is generous... It is an area for experts, and I can only offer fairly limited advice.

During those ghastly opening salvos, the dreaded and emotive M word is bound to prove an ongoing flashpoint for both of you. Crudely, you have now got half of however much money you had before, as you are now attempting to run two households out of the same pot. This always seems to be the case, even if the Other Woman has her own job, country cottage and fleet of vehicles. How can you and he work this out amicably when there is so much acrimony in the mix already?

Dementing about money and suddenly having less money than you are used to notches up all the post-dumpage insecurity still more. At a time when you most need to be engulfed in and insulated by endless treats, you are being required to economise and scrimp, for Christ's sake.

I remember seeing red each time my ex appeared in a swanky unfamiliar sweater or brand new hiking boots. It was intolerable staring down at his expensive shiny feet, blinking away tears of impotent rage while he pompously explained that he could not contribute to our son's school trip or birthday party.

Ten years on (when there is much less friction, as I have got used to paying for almost everything), I still feel ratty when my son tells me that my supposedly totally impecunious ex has splashed out thirty quid on a special occasions cookbook! What? This is the man who claims he is not ever in a position to contribute to his children's hobbies or extra-curricular events. He occasionally buys them nice clothes, but of course it's more fun buying your boys treatish bits and bobs on a whim than coughing up regularly for the ugly, dullsville school stuff that they are not remotely bothered about but have to have.

No, I can't think of much remotely positive to say on the subject of money post the break-up except that it is not possible to go on feeling angry at full pelt indefinitely. Fretting about money is a corrosive and unrewarding pastime day in day out. You will end up even boring yourself by worrying about it incessantly, and regrettably it is almost impossible not to contaminate the kids with your many money bitternesses at least sometimes:

'*The reason we can't go to Pizza Express anymore is that we can't afford it (though your dad seems able to go on endless expensive foreign holidays with his new family).*'
Or:

'*Could you tell your dad for a change instead of me that your trainers are leaking and that you are the only boy in the class without a phone?*'

You can try threats, emotional blackmail and all sorts, but usually to no avail. There is never enough money to go round and he will categorically refuse to favour you over his new situation. If he was able to put you and the kids first the likelihood is that he would not have dumped you in the first place. When he is being startlingly stingy you can at least be quite open to friends and relatives about the levels of his contributions and that might shame him into a bit of action. Men tend not to like people perceiving them as mean.

A close friend's husband was a successful accountant who made his living from making a lot look like a little on paper and she had absolutely no chance of getting a fair deal from him. What is a fair deal anyway, in the end? No one seems able to agree on this. Or rather dumped women agree with other dumped women, as do dumping men with their new partners, and there is always a massive gulf between the two camps.

The truth is that you will only be spared the additional horror of arguing over money if you have major means of your own. Keep going, though. And remember – independence, in this respect, is king. If you've got a job, hang on to it! There is only one happy place to be vis-à-vis money, if you ask me, and that's not having to ask for it.

Strategies – yours, and how best to counter some of his

Access and money are probably the worst of your specific problems in the early stages after dumpage. But as time goes on there will be endless to-ing and fro-ing between you and your ex about almost every aspect of the children's lives. For this you need to be armed and prepared. So, I thought it as well here to offer just a quick note on strategy in general. (Definition of: '*The art of a commander-in-chief; the art of projecting and directing the larger military movements and operations of a campaign.*')

Power balances are tricky in any relationship, but especially between exes. Men often behave as if they are still in charge after the separation, and go on acting as though they still live on site. It can take some time for the reality of their own departure to catch up with them. He may, for example, try to:

a) Force you to commit to decisions with regard to the children's holidays, schooling, diet, bedtimes or haircuts that you are either not ready to take or not happy about taking, when with no warning he suddenly wants everything finalised. (The Bolter used regularly to have the boys' heads shaved without consulting me or them and there seemed to be nothing I could do, no threat in the world to stop it, even though he knew how hideous everyone except him thought it made them look.)

b) Get so angry when things are not as easy as he anticipated that he threatens to opt out all together. That one is very common. The Bolter once stayed out of touch for six months for exactly that reason. I finally cracked and rang him when the elder child decided he must have died.

c) Accuse you of being selfish and obstructive and making things more difficult for the kids.

With regard to absolutely all of this, sweet reason – and I mention in passing a female definition of this that I like and approve of, '*to think in a connected, sensible or logical manner*' – is one of your perfect counter-strategies.

Calm reasonableness really can be your ally. In the early days everything seems so desperately hard and I have yelled, sworn, screamed and thrown things with the best of them. When, on the odd occasion, though, and then more and more, I have managed to counter his irrational rants and threats with sturdy, unharried restatements of salient facts it has proved extremely satisfying and occasionally even silenced him.

When, for example, my ex used to yell that he 'needed' to see his children, I would reply in my most saccharinely pious voice:

'*I believe it was your "needs" that took you away from your children in the first place. The problem is that your "needs" seem to be rather in conflict with each other.*'

Sometimes, you can turn the control-freakery back on him and have a bit of fun by getting on that phone.

'Hi Deirdre, I'm really sorry to bother you, but Philip was always very keen that Tristram finished his maths before he watched The Simpsons. The thing is he's got stuck with the last question so I wondered if Philip could either help him solve it over the phone or relax that particular rule. I really don't want to undermine Philip's position on this one as he did seem to feel so very strongly about it when he still lived here. No, if you could ask him and get back to me that would be terrifically helpful. Thank you so much. I'll ring back again if I may if anything else crops up this evening. Byeeeeeeeeeeeee.'

After several evenings of this type of 'concerned' intervention, your ex is likely to decide that he is much too busy with his new life to be consulted over this level of detail. Fine. Then, when he next massively disapproves of some decision you have made without consulting him, you can regretfully lob that extreme busyness back in his face.

Every now and then actually being nice can work very well, too. Early on I would never concede anything on principle, so when I started to give in graciously, very occasionally, he was totally thrown. Think ahead to what suits you and then appear to slot in generously with what he wants without his realising that his plans happen to suit you.

And then, eventually, some of the heat seeps out of the situation and you weary of taking swings at each other over every last detail. It is a tiny thing but when my younger son asked me recently:

'Do you think my dad would mind if I didn't stay with him when I've got exams as I'd rather be at home?'

I said I thought it would be fine. I was, of course, pleased that he was quite so clear that this was his actual home, in spite of his father's superior cooking skills which both boys regularly tease me about. I was also relieved that my ex and I were now finally on sufficiently bearable terms for this modest request not to explode into a major trauma involving, as it did, a change of access in my favour. And that now does feel a better place to be.

Paranoia over your kids' behaviour

You will undoubtedly experience major angst with regard to your children's newly acquired habits of scowling, wetting their beds, being rude, playing you off against their dad, etc, etc, as a result of your ex shipping off into his rose-tinted shag-fest of a new life. He has other preoccupations now, and will be reluctant to involve himself in the emotional chaos he is leaving behind.

The first thing to focus on is the soothing fact that children behave badly and are ill-mannered even when their dads do not leave. I still remember my mean-spirited relief when my six-year-old nephew started 'soiling' himself at nursery. There did not seem to be any reason and it went on for weeks and weeks to major consternation.

The child's parents were close and loving, the family had a nice home, no financial worries, good health and this boy's dad had absolutely no intention of abandoning him. There was no obvious cause, not a single cloud that anyone was aware of on that family's horizon and the nursery staff and immediate family were all baffled. If it had been my son, though, I would have been unshakeably convinced it was related to the hideous old dad-leaving-trauma and nothing could have changed that mindset. This is one of the many difficulties you will find yourself facing with regard to your children's behaviour after you have been dumped. It is impossible to work out what exactly causes which symptom when.

Boys, especially, can wet their beds for years. One of mine did and the other never did. Was one of them more affected by his dad leaving than the other? I will never know, and thank God, really, for that but the time I emphatically thought it was one of many signs that my son would never ever recover from his father's abrupt departure.

I tormented myself worrying that he would never be able to go on sleepovers or have girlfriends or boyfriends or go anywhere ever for the rest of his life. In fact I was in total despair about the whole situation. The star charts had not worked and making him change the sheets, wash them and remake his bed had not worked and then suddenly he stopped and never ever wet his bed again.

What can I say? Now I barely remember it and neither does he and in retrospect I wish to God I hadn't muddled it all up in my own head to quite such a degree with his Dad leaving, as gratuitously linking the two things in that way simply notched up everyone's already rampaging stress levels!

Nearly all kids are bolshy, needy, secretive and stroppy at different stages in their lives. It is a part of growing up and forging an identity and gaining independence from you that everyone goes through. You, though, as a dumped mum feel fabulously vulnerable socially when your kids misbehave. You imagine that people must be tutting behind your back about the havoc that the split-up has wreaked on the children, about your weakness in being unable to control them by yourself, and so on and so forth. You fear that your children are manifesting their deep misery at having separated parents by their tight-lipped refusals to say thank you for juice.

Do try not to obsess about this as there are so many different conflicting factors that govern children's behaviour. I am not dismissing the significance of dads and their leaving and the way that they leave and all of that. I do feel now, though, with the benefit of hindsight, that I made myself miserable to the point of being ill by attributing every single behavioural aberration manifested by my growing kids to the departure of their father. Added to which, other parents were usually too preoccupied with worrying about their own children's tics to be critical of mine.

Thinking about it carefully now, I know rude children and nice children and it does not in any way neatly correlate with whether or not their parents have split up. Genes, position in the family, the behaviour of siblings, peers, success or not at school, all of those things have a bearing as well, and you try to separate out causes of this and that and respective significances at your peril.

That said, one of the worst aspects of the whole experience of being dumped is watching your kids suffer. You feel so damned impotent; for me anyway, it registered as the first time I really could not fix things for them. If they were hungry I had fed them, tired, I had stuck them in bed, grazed knee, I would do sympathetic plaster acting, but in these circumstances, their anguish destroyed me afresh because I could not do a thing to make it better for them, not a thing.

I also remember my feelings of helplessness in the early days after the split when my boys battened on other children's jolly, bulky dads at parties or in the park. The rueful kindness and patience of these men, whether or not they were aware of my kids' situation, made me sick with regret. I found it impossible not to feel desperate about what my children were missing and how it might affect them, this failure of mine, even though it was not my fault, to provide them with what they properly deserved and what other kids around them had. This acute sadness does ease, though, I promise and, if it does not pass entirely, it does definitely transmogrify into different emotions.

Nine years in, I watch my boys' adolescent peers at odds with both their parents, and am fairly confident that in the single mum homes there tends to be less conflict. There are probably fewer rows, as there are fewer combinations to finesse. It is not a better environment — I am certainly not claiming that — but I think perhaps as a single-mum one can sometimes be more subtle, more reactive, more flexible with regard to growing children's needs. There are areas with regard to my boys' behaviour that my ex has always felt very strongly about, and he is not wrong necessarily, but he is unremittingly hardline. Kids need boundaries but they also need unexpected treats, and affirmation. However much two parents discuss rules and eventualities, they are bound to differ and diverge on some issues and that always causes difficulties. It is much easier to be inconsistent in a good way if there is only one of you.

If the kids live with you, whatever the access arrangements, I reckon you have the right both to make the rules and bask in the compliments if your kids behave well. Those compliments and that pleasure in your children's good behaviour, then, is the upside of your paranoia about their bad behaviour after the split.

A few weeks after his father had left, my four-year-old had a screaming fit on the doorstep when his dad turned up to collect him.

'*You're not my father anymore so you can't tell me what to do!*'

Then he stormed off upstairs to his room and slammed the door, leaving my ex-partner angrily flustered and unsure how best to react. My son's bad behaviour had been occasioned by the dumping undoubtedly, but there was a truth at the heart of it which a small part of me relished. I knew that I did still have the right to tell my son what to do as I had not left and had not forfeited any of my rights. In that respect, for a change, I was infinitely better placed than his dad.

If you travel alone you get exposed to more than if you travel with a partner, and I think if you bring up children pretty much by yourself, they get exposed to more in a good way as well as to the obvious bad things. Of course, you do not want to be a drag on your children, or martyrish, but sometimes your legitimate tiredness or sorrow is good for them to see and react to, and obviously cannot simply be filed under:

'*Oh, yawn, Mum's fed up; Dad can deal with it.*'

I have had the most blissful birthdays ever, when I know categorically that the funny little scraps of paper, gestures and breakfast trays have been done solo without the help of another adult on the sidelines. On

Mother's Day, I view with amusement bordering on pity the procession of self-important dads from the flower shop down the road, cradling expensive bouquets and dragging bored children along the pavement. Yes, on this day I pity the smug nuclears, I do; and I treasure whatever small funniness I have been given. There is a big difference after all between:

'We ought to get your mother some flowers'
and:

'Mum, this is for you'

These days I never feel remotely tragic on my birthday or Mother's day. Not one whit.

This next point may be borderline, but perhaps worth trying to articulate even so. The dynamic in a single-mum household can, I think, leave the kids a bit more air and space to take the initiative and help out, without it simply being a question of trying to get them to do the chores because they are so flipping spoilt and should do more. My kids will click visiting friends' babies into car seats and shove pushchairs into the boot unbidden, largely because it means that we will get to where we are going more quickly – but it's still heartening. They also pack shopping at the supermarket with gusto and seem quite naturally to assume responsibility for stuff around the house, even if that means water fights in the guise of watering the garden.

It is much nicer for me than my having to whinge at an often preoccupied dad that neither he nor they do enough to help me. It is quite a thrill when your kids do some dull chore or other without being asked simply because they sense that you are up against it or fed up, or both. Quite often it is exactly those things — taking out the bin, cleaning the rubbish out of the car, playing with the baby so you can read the Sunday papers — that my friends wear themselves out trying to get their husbands to do.

And, finally, a word about just the relative anal-ness and competitiveness of men — which seems some-how much more rampant and potent in your average nuclear family. Quite soon after my kids' father had left, my son was invited over to play at rather a grand house. When I arrived to pick up my child, the mum took me aside and hissed apologetically that her hus-band had been rather difficult all day even though she had pleaded with him to be jolly:

'Daniel, this little boy comes from a broken home. We must give him a nice time.'

Reeling somewhat from this unexpected perspec-tive on the horror that must be my son's life, I popped him into the car and, as we drove away, asked him if he had had a good time.

'*It was OK, but the dad kept telling us not to do things.*'

'*Like what?*'

'*Oh, you know, stuff like don't smash the plants with that football and this is a brand new car so please be careful. He didn't seem to want us to do anything.*'

As he spoke, my son was tramping mud merrily all over the back seat. We had all thought it was hilarious when our glossy new car had got badly scratched by one of the boy's bicycles falling against it on the day we got it. I bet you anything a husband or partner, or my son's friend's dad, might not however have found that particular incident quite as side-splitting.

In my experience, most single mums are far less anal about their cars, computers and possessions generally, than most married dads. And sometimes, bizarrely, even in the most classically, this-is-a-dad's-thang scenario, your kids can have a better time with you. I once took my boys to a wonderful vehicle-building event at the Science Museum and was, of course, pretty much the only mum there. Having had the foresight to acquire both the Sunday papers and a monster cappuccino, I settled down for a blissful couple of hours, as did my boys with endless nice staff dancing attendance on them, while all the other children watched sadly from the sidelines as their competitive dads wrenched any remaining vehicles out of tiny hands, shouting:

'No, Dominic — it's a reverse camber. Let ME do it please!'

When you are feeling particularly paranoid about your kids' behaviour in the savage aftermath of the split, I hope you can comfort yourself slightly with some of the above. If you have boys they will definitely end up more compassionate; and the girls will be less self-centred too.

Phone calls

How on earth can phone calls throw you off course now that you are well on your way and even starting to enjoy the view for the first time?

Actually, phone calls can prove damnably tricky. For me, and I suspect a number of other single mums, the telephone as an imagined or supposed link with the absent loved/hated/desperately missed father can be pretty unsettling. Talking to their dad on the phone appeared seductive to the children early on, but invariably ended up being fraught with misunderstandings.

Phones promise the possibility of contact, but

don't really deliver. I wish now that I had had a clearer sense of this at the time. The Bolter, for example, had a habit of telling his sons he would phone over the weekend and then somehow not getting around to it. My sons would circle round and round the phone unwilling to go to the park or have a bath in case they missed him.

This was obviously pre-mobiles, but a lot of the same difficulties still obtain or indeed are magnified now that most people do. There is NO conceivable reason for him not to ring us, is there? Well, being on the job, to name but eight! Our phone came to seem like an evil black beast that was resolutely refusing to play with my kids or humour them by shrilling. Then, when finally it did ring after hours of nightmarish anticipation, it was inevitably someone suggesting we try a different gas company or a colleague of mine with a query, and the children would be totally deflated and the whole ghastly cycle would start again.

On the occasions when their dad did manage to ring his kids on the day he had said he might, they would never really know what to say or how to cope with my hissed and out-of-synch promptings in the background. Once this hysterically anticipated phone call had finally taken place we would all be left empty and confused. As for me, I tended to feel horribly cheated; that the boys had never satisfactorily been able to convey to him quite how miserably dark it was for us all living right down in the bottom of doom valley.

'*They sound fine to me,*'

...would invariably be their father's complacent response.

'*Never better.*'

I think you have, if you will forgive the expression, to get on top of the phone. Dumping dads vary in their preferences for communicating or not with their kids by phone, but things did perk up slightly when I decided we were not going to hang about and stay in waiting for possible calls. And somehow I managed to carry the children with me on this. Certainly, we received our fair share of inconveniently timed calls ourselves. How many miserable mums have suffered the endless to-ing and fro-ing of, '*Is Dad going to phone?*' and then the call finally coming just when it's least convenient. We always seemed to be eating our evening meal more or less happily when their father would call (an invariably hunched, wan conversation, punctuated by: '*When can we see you?*' or '*Will you be able to collect me from school tomorrow?*'), and they would push their cold food away, saying dismally that they did not feel hungry anymore.

Then they remember that they are in fact hungry when they are in bed. They cannot get to sleep and insist on going through all the things they had been saving up to tell him but forgot at the crucial juncture. In the interim it has got horribly late and they are all hopped up and your evening is in tatters yet again.

Basically, in so far as it is remotely possible, you need to answer the phone and return his calls in a way that suits you and the kids. Tell him when he should ring. Obviously, older kids will have mobiles, and maybe you have one and do not mind being available to him at all times, but for what it is worth I found it to be debilitating. I needed to take control, otherwise the phone was like a little port that could open unexpectedly and bleed more sadness and loss back into my life when I was not properly protected. If he is horrible or brisk when you are feeling bad it is hard, and if he is nice and patient and sympathetic it is worse because he has left now and is probably being even nicer and kinder and more sympathetic to someone else. Ouch.

My view is that I should have made it clear from

the start that the telephone was only really of use for arrangements. I never once remember a bedtime call that left my children feeling happier and more settled – and, above all, more 'thought of' – in the early days anyway. As for you, unless you are ridiculously vigilant, a key phone call with him to discuss routines and precedents that are hugely important to you to get right, almost always comes just as the children are playing up and the dog is barking and the milk is boiling over and the smoke alarm is going off. You can flipping well imagine him glorying in your confusion as the floozie in a fetching designer top rolls her eyes sympathetically and hands him a clinking gin and tonic while whipping up a delectable little snack for two.

On the power front, however, phone calls can also be a way of your withholding for a change. You are not under any obligation to answer the phone unless you have agreed that you would at a certain time. Why should you haul them out of their baths when he rings out of the blue, suddenly feeling sentimental at the end of a difficult day in the office? After a number of extremely stressful phone exchanges between our respective households, my ex made the cardinal error of getting his wife to tell me that he did not want to speak to me or the children again that night. That was a real error of judgement on his part, as we then did not phone him for weeks so his only way of communicating was to keep trying us until we elected to pick up.

You can also on occasion use the telephone quite effectively as a weapon yourself. I wish now that I had rung rather more often at four in the morning instead of only occasionally, and very nervously, at six, when my two-year-old had already been awake for hours crying piteously for his dad. (This was tiring as his brother used to have his 'missing Dad' sobbing fits at midnight or one.)

What I could not bear, though, was the thought of having to speak to her. I used to feel sick with horrified anticipation that she might answer the phone and that I would actually have to share the ether with her. The sound of her voice was repulsive to me – bogus and terrifyingly intriguing. Hearing her murmur hello would rip me up as I thought somehow that the inflection and the volume could provide me with a key as to why he was so absurdly attracted to her.

Related to that was the visceral revulsion I felt when people rang my number and asked for her – which did happen on several occasions. I felt contaminated and screamed incontinently at the hapless caller on the other end. As for my ex, for years and years afterwards people still rang and asked for him and it is only relatively recently that I have felt able to reply sensibly.

Leaving a message can also be useful as a way of communicating. If there are ongoing dates or issues that are under dispute I found that it often suited me to leave a firm, clear message – having called when I knew they were going to be out – so as to avoid getting into a wrangle and ending up shouting, or crying, or worst of all backing down.

On a few occasions, I must own up, I left abusive messages; but to be honest I don't really regret those intemperate blasts of:

'This is how it is for us right now because of your willy-centric actions'.

If the dumpers choose to, they can delete your misery without even listening to it; you, however, do not have that option. Why yet again is there one set of rules for them, and another for you? It may not be particularly festive for them to come back from a cosy dinner à deux to rants on the answer machine, but neither is the situation particularly jolly for you. The answer message is a temporary way at least of crashing the desperate reality of his rejected life into his pleasurable new existence, and there can be, yes, let us admit it, just a modicum of solace in that. It is called I think, turning into the skid!

Illness

You really are starting to get on top of things now as you speed on through and illness and fatigue are your last irritants in this *Drizzle and road bumps* section

When he first goes, of course, you cannot even begin to sleep or eat and I seemed to go deaf as well, almost literally! I would come to with a crash when the children finally resorted to shaking me. Then I would mentally replay the last few minutes or half an hour, or whatever it was, realising to my horror that a child had been asking me for something over and over again. I had totally blanked them out as I was hermetically preoccupied with more pressing issues, like:

What is the best and most effective way of ruining both of their lives?

Hard as it is, do try to look after yourself. With your sleeping, eating, relaxing and exercising patterns all totally gone to pot, you are in danger of getting badly run down and picking up every bug around — something you do not need on top of all the other traumas that you are trying to negotiate.

It is now generally accepted that exercise releases endorphins which physiologically counter depression. Obviously a little bike ride or joggette is not going to sort out all your problems and pop the world back to a sunny state of hunkydoryness over night but I do know categorically that a walk with the kids or a swim by yourself is not going to make you feel any worse. It can only help, however slightly, with the lack-of-sleeping misery and is a healthier way of losing weight than the ongoing feeling-sick-and-not-wanting-to-eat state. Being outdoors in the sun and looking at the sea or clouds might just distract you, if only for a few seconds.

Several years after The Bolter had left, I developed abdominal pains and ongoing nausea. I was checked out for every conceivable ailment and in the end the nice hospital doctor, who knew nothing of my recent history, gently told me that these symptoms were very common in people who had experienced some kind of major life trauma three to four years earlier. I was stunned that I could be inflicting something this unpleasant on myself and felt like a fraud and a hypochondriac but I also did slowly start to get better. Bear in mind that you really are running on empty and it may be that you think you can cope indefinitely as you know that you have to, but some physical symptoms might bulge out sideways and take you unawares.

Try to eat good things as well as the desperately needed comfort stuff if, that is, you have got a mind to eat at all. I remember being unable to swallow anything for days on end and felt sick whenever I went past the fridge. I had bought a beautiful sea bass for The Bolter to cook as part of the last shop I had done for two. He had gone before that meal actually took place, and, unsurprisingly I could not then face the fish alone.

I immediately gave my foodie brother the offending item, but still the fridge came to represent raw, unwanted, oppressive, expensive sea bass to me. With this odious fish trauma weighing heavily on my appetite, I could only contemplate mashed potato or sliced banana for weeks, probably because that was what my mum used to give us when we were convalescent or delicate.

Immediately after you have been dumped, though, you do need vitamins more than ever, just to give you the energy to get up in the morning, preferably in the form of blueberries, avocados, kiwis and broccoli, those so-called super vegetables or whatever they are.

Get yourself nice nuts to nibble even if you cannot yet face whole meals. When I suspected a recently dumped friend of mine had not been eating properly, I invited her round, relaxed her with lashings of wine and made her a luxury small salad. Then I made her laugh so that she did not notice that she was eating it, a bit of colour came back into her face and she did admit just fleetingly to feeling a fraction more optimistic. Added to which, if you do not eat or barely eat, that dragging fatigue which is pulling you down to the depths will get worse and worse.

You also need to keep an eye on your mental health. What can help you to heal?

The simple fact of time elapsing and distancing you from the break-up does slowly help to ease some of that pain. If you imagine the longest as opposed to the shortest conceivable time it will take you to feel just fractionally better, then you might surprise yourself.

Talk about it. You want and need and have to talk about what has happened, and how you feel, and how unfair it is and what he had the gall to say when he picked up the kids last Thursday... over and over again. It is one of the few releases you have got for the confusion and sorrow bubbling around in your head all day, and most of the night as well. It is normal to want to talk about it, but however nice and supportive your friends are, they will get bored, and that is where, if you can afford it, paying someone to listen to you comes in.

I sought professional help when I noticed my friends changing the subject each time I mentioned 'him' or ' her' or 'them'. Irritatingly they did not seem to want to devote any more long afternoons to that one all-absorbing and endlessly circular subject. I was far from talked out, however, so I got a therapist with an ugly, grey pudding-bowl haircut who never laughed at my jokes and talked at her instead for about eighteen months.

If you do not feel inclined to talk to a stranger, or have not got the time or the money, then try and ring the changes if you can with regard to whom you talk to on the family, friends, neighbours and colleagues front. I remember, when my sister was being dumped, being on an informal family rota for lengthy evening phone calls. People who have been dumped them-selves are likely to be more tolerant of the minutiae but do try, however hard it seems, to be aware that you will have become slightly obsessive.

I remember with a cold sweat the lunch hour I spent sobbing in a chilly stairwell at work on the shoulder of someone whom I had not seen for a while. When she finally stood up with difficulty to go back to work, I belatedly asked her how she was doing, and she said that she had recently had a life-threatening physical collapse.

My ranting, self-pitying monologue had prevented me from even noticing she was under the weather, until it was too late to sympathise or hear her story properly. At that stage it did dawn on me that my own sadness was making me insensitive to other people to a degree that was wholly unacceptable.

On another occasion, I was in such full flow with another mum about the 'Other Woman' that I failed to notice my toddler climbing out of his pushchair, pottering quite some distance to the park gates and stepping out onto a busy hill between parked cars. Thank Christ he was all right but there were screeching brakes and understandably ratty drivers. You do need to talk and exorcise stuff but it can easily get out of hand and blind you to the basic requirements of your day-to-day existence.

As well as retelling your woes endlessly to whoever you can collar, you also need repeatedly to churn everything over by yourself. That is how it was for me anyway. I found my new situation so indigestibly incomprehensible, that I needed to chew it and chew it in my head. I used to welcome long car journeys for that reason, knowing that, having spent the entire drive in agonised introspection, I might, with luck, be a few millimetres nearer to calm and sanity on arrival.

In my view nothing in the world can really make the pain of being dumped better or easier to negotiate. But some activities might just help you move through it all without getting stuck in a hopeless swamp of bitterness. I felt the need to write hundreds of angry letters, most of which I think The Bolter discarded on arrival, as during a fraught phone call with his new wife she told me that he invariably tossed any letters from me straight into the bin unread. Even so, writing stuff down did give me some respite from the incessant circular whirring of all those injustices in my head. It helped me to try to set events down in some kind of shape and order. If you are a private person and do not care to talk publicly about your traumas, then maybe filling up notebooks will help.

Fatigue

Fatigue is meshed in with all of this health mullarkey and some of the dictionary definitions are spot on, given that the tiredness you are experiencing is likely to be mental and emotional, as well as physical.

Fatigued: *sick of, weary of, impatient with, exhausted, worked out, used up*.

Yup, and triple yup. All of that seems as familiar as the stack of dirty saucepans and the overflowing laundry basket. You are tired of your situation, wearied by it and all used up by being the sole carer for your kids most of the time. But there is a kind of upside. This section is not just an elongated whinge. No. We are now actually starting to look ahead.

When 'it' first happens, decent, life-giving, normal sleep will hurtle straight out of the window. You can almost see the good sleep figure packing his bags and marching off behind your partner!

I have canvassed many women on the subject of fatigue and it undoubtedly constitutes one of our major fears. Everyone laughs nervously about the mum who was so tired she sprinkled sweets in her toddler's cot so that when he woke in the night he would find them and eat them rather than cry for her. Most of us, though, have fantasised about similarly inappropriate solutions to the ongoing fatigue trauma. Lack of sleep stalks us, scares us, makes us snap at the children, makes our hair go lank, makes us fear with reason that if we work or try to work we will no longer be able to do our jobs properly, and, in fact, totally threatens our well-being. This sapping exhaustion can really seem like the final straw. However, I can say categorically and with a certain measure of... yes, pleasure actually, that further down the line the established single mums often seem less tired than those nuclear mums enjoying secure coupledom!

On the face of it, this assertion may seem absurd. There is only one of you, and there are two parents in other families and even if, guess what, the dad does less than the mum, do the math, as they say in America.

The truth is, though, that while there are two of them and one of you with the same amount of responsibility and thingage to get through – meals to cook, football matches to drive to, swings to push, and on and on and on – oddly the single mums seem to have a couple of advantages over their partnered counterparts. For a start, they expend absolutely zero energy on wishing their partners did more. Single mums never waste time wondering:

'Why does it never occur to him to take out the bloody kitchen bin?'

It would be ludicrous to accord that query any brain space when the couch potato in question is now cosily ensconced with his new floozy in a love nest. With any luck, it is now that floozy who in her turn is wondering ruefully...

'Why on earth can't he ever be arsed to rinse out the bath/put the loo seat down/hang up the damp towels?'

I have yet to come across a nuclear family where the partners share the domestic and parenting chores equally, even when they both have demanding jobs outside the home.

It does not happen. It just does not. So, given it never happens, and almost invariably it is the benighted mums who do more – worry about the packed lunches, or the absence of clean school shirts or the mysteriously mislaid swimmers – then those mums have to be superhuman saints not to be thinking just sometimes: why is it always me?

Every single one of my nice, ostensibly happily married female friends bends my ear from time to time about the lack of support they get from their more or less decent husbands in some area or other relating to the home, their kids, or their careers. And

I believe that the sort of resentment us dumped mums feel about our situation is genuinely less sapping than the knowledge that you have to do it all, even though there is another adult there under your nose, opting out, reading the paper, having a beer, making stupid excuses and getting narky and calling you a nag if you moan.

In addition, the single mums can go to bed at eight if they feel like it, after a zonking bubble bath with a shlocky magazine, the cordless phone and the biggest glass of wine you have ever seen. They do not have to cook and wash up for their partner or hear about his day and his meeting and the fact he was robbed at squash or, worst of absolutely all, climb into a shimmering number and slap on the slap for a corporate dinner. I know that is part and parcel of being in a relationship but all of those requirements can be quite tiring at the end of a long day. There aren't many husbands I know who encourage their wives scrap supper and yack on the phone for hours and watch crap telly all evening. Sometimes, though, that is exactly what you need to do.

One friend of mine, who works and has three kids, has a partner who was always away travelling in far-flung parts of the globe and she learnt to function pretty effectively as a quasi-single mum. Recently, though, her husband has been out of work a lot, mooching about at home. He still seems unable – or rather unwilling – to take on any of her domestic duties. He is unused to shouldering any of that particular load and, dement as she does, she just cannot get him to help, even though she is patently wiped out working full-time and running the house. She has made some headway recently. She has stopped ironing his shirts, leaving them to mount up on the landing for everyone to step over. One night she put supper in the oven and went off for a swim and came back to find the rest of her family watching the football and starving, with the forgotten meal in cinders in the oven. She has screamed with the stress of trying to climb into smart clothes for work while giving the baby breakfast, as her partner will not change his own hallowed morning bath routine.

Now I would find all of this quite debilitating and she agrees that on balance she often feels she is more tired than me – not least because he snores and she usually has to retire to a futon on the bathroom floor to get any kip.

Feeling tired? Go to bed and the next day with any luck you might feel less tired. (This, I must stress, is when you are well into your single-mum treadmill and not in the suicidal, all-over-the-place throes of those first, hellish, sleep-free few months.) As an established single mum it is pretty unlikely, after all, that you will be entertaining non-stop or going out six nights in a row, so once the kids are fed and bedded you have only got yourself to please. It can be lonely, but gazooks it can also be lusciously gratifying when you are sane enough to enjoy it.

When The Bolter, before he had bolted, tried to avoid coming out to play with the kids, I would feel tired by his reluctance and tired by my own attempts to shame him into coming. Then I would feel deeply, deeply tired at having to yomp off in a huff with the kids to a grey, boring park, purely on principle, while he relaxed with the Sunday papers and forgot to prepare any lunch. Of course, there are nice, plaid weekend dads knocking around who skip joyfully out to the park with children, a football, frisbee and roller-blades at the drop of a hat but, for all of those, there are at least as many who fall into the category described above.

Outwitting ambushes
You have got the radio tuned to your favourite station,

you're doing well, yes, you actually feel OK…

Hold onto your hat, though; for, just when you think it is safe to relax into the next phase of your journey, you may well be entering prime ambush territory where unhelpful memories, anniversaries, in-jokes and old family rituals can suddenly leap out at you.

Christmas is a prime example of a potential lurking ambush. If you have got the kids, for heaven's sake try not to let any aspects or memories of past Christmases creep up on you unawares, and then depress you and unhinge you and blow that festive spirit to bits. This is a time of year littered with emotional land-mines.

I remember the year The Bolter had shipped out, overhearing my son, when asked by his cousins what he wanted for Christmas, replying that there was only one thing that he wanted in the world – his dad back.

That cast a long black shadow over the entire season and was not something I could easily solve, even by resorting to my overstretched credit card. Whether you are a planning kind of person or a spontaneous go-with-the-flow type, post-relationship meltdown, it is probably worth organising things like crazy to avoid being assaulted by misery over that Christmas period. Friends, expeditions, treats, and lashings of planning really can help here. There is no harm at all in judiciously and artificially distracting yourself and the kids from the memories and the pain of it all at those times when you think that you might be badly placed to cope.

I will never forget trying to hide tears from my excited small son who was buying his first proper pencil case and all the bits and bobs to go in it prior to starting at big school. I felt so bloody bleak at this key moment in the emotional trajectory of my eldest child, so alone and sad and hard done by that I could hardly walk up to the cashier without melting into a pool of self-pity at the feet of the other shoppers. I should have gone with a mate or a relative, who could have enthused about novelty rubbers and made an event of it.

'What fun this is... how about those felt pens over there?'

...as opposed to,

'Why is it that this sad little expedition most epitomises the dashing of all my hopes for my family forever?'

If you are spending Christmas without your kids you need to plan even more carefully at first. You may have family around eager to scoop you up but just consider for a moment whether or not you are really ready to engage with their children's festive excitement when you have not got your own kids around opening stockings. Maybe it would be better for you to do something completely different with a childless friend – a trip to a health club or hotel or a mini-break abroad to somewhere very hot or intensely cold depending on your mood. You really can learn to anticipate and swerve round some of these upturned nails in the road before they bring you to a grinding halt.

The first evening ever, for example, that the kids are with him and, gulp, her, you must plan at the very minimum to get manageably pissed before going to a stupid movie with a sane mate, which means with any luck that you will only feel suicidal intermittently. Do not just think:

'Oh I'll stay in. It'll be fine. I'm knackered after all and it'll be great to have the house to myself and God knows the airing cupboard needs tidying. Good, that's settled then.'

No, no, no. It will be irredeemably ghastly and you will feel terrible and pad from room to room and feel unable to go anywhere near that airing cupboard. Get out there and use the money that you are saving on a babysitter for an extra treat.

Do not be thrown by those Saturday mornings either, when you always used to have a big jolly family brunch. If, for example, he always wielded the frying pan and wore a silly chef's hat, it will certainly be a mistake to try to recreate it without him. Institute something else, something mildly treatish for the kids perhaps, but different.

Actually when you are ambushed for no obvious reason by your feelings because – well, just because of what has happened and is happening and you are tired of being brave, and it is not because the kids are with him, or that it is your birthday – then is a good time to do horrid airing-cupboard tidying for the sake of it. It sops up the time until you start to feel better. You cannot usually feel that level of misery for days on end, and instead of curling up and frowsting weepily in an armchair you will at least have a surge of pride at your achievement in creating a pristine and celestial glory hole under the stairs. That is the plan anyway as when you feel lousy for no reason, doing nothing can often make you feel worse.

This may sound a bit anal but I recommend a moment one morning when you are feeling relatively upbeat to make a handy list of phone numbers of people you can comfortably call on for different things. Then, when you are fraught and knackered and have raging PMT, as happened to me recently, when even with the text-book open at the explanations page and spurred on by elder son's despair, the quadratic equations homework still spun before my eyes and the supper did not get started and my head throbbed and I felt totally ambushed by my pathetic innumeracy... What would I have given to be able to say calmly to my son:

'Here are three numerate grown-ups to ring who will happily talk you through it after supper when we are all feeling a bit stronger.'

In the early days of the break-up, when you are in a state, and you encounter things that you absolutely cannot do, things that symbolise brawny male absence, be it changing a tyre or a even a bloody light bulb because the casing thing snaps, then the fact of your lonely, vulnerable ineptitude can gouge deep tracks through your soul. The thing, unachieved, haunts you for days, shouting at you that you are a failure on every front, and everyone gets fed up with having to brush their teeth in the dark.

When people offer to help, they do not usually mean, let us have the kids for a few weeks in the summer while you go and relax in San Tropez with your new lover; but they do often want to do something, and helping in some small way may well also make them feel good. So, when the wives with DIY hubbies offer general support, don't turn them down in some unnecessary show of independence. (Remember to be sensitive about how you ask and what for, as even the best of friends do not want to feel that you are hitting on their preening Black and Decker husbands under the pretext of fine-tuning the stereo. You do, of course, discover post-dumpage that you can do a lot more than you thought you could. But some things – heavy lifting to name but eight – will remain obstinately outside any amount of new empowerment.)

For the first few years after my partner left, all my memories of him upset me. I could not recall a single thing we had done together that did not make me feel miserable when I remembered it.

Now, though, when I think back to his reactions to the birth of our first child all of those years ago, I can actually smile quietly and enjoy it again, most of the time. I no longer feel patronised and beaten by the Other Woman in his life. I sometimes even feel superior to her because I know categorically that he did not have his first ever child with her, and that situation can never change, and that is cool and nice and something I will always have over her. Yes, now I really do feel pretty much OK that he was there and he loved both his babies at the time, even though it all went horribly wrong frighteningly soon after those doting hospital pictures were taken.

Sometimes I would deliberately summon up those 'birth' memories when he was making cruel claims about our past life together and the fact that we had not been close for ages... Although those memories could not really change my situation they were a small solace to me, a reassurance on occasion that he was the one going mad not me, forgetting the utter bliss that such moments really had been.

I have also, since the bust-up, had occasion to be firm with myself and summon less good memories to help me through. This is a complicated one. Sometimes on a 'family' holiday, alone with the boys, I felt so wronged and cheated I would have to remind myself to interrogate the past as it really had been, rather than in terms of sentimental and unreal picture-book memories.

Family holidays were not frankly one of The Bolter's great strengths. He loved picnics on the sadly few family holidays we did achieve before he left but he was generally pretty unsociable and always brought lots of work with him. And to be honest, when I recall those days as they actually were, I do not feel that gutted to have lost him. There are times, then, when memories can assist you, reminding you that these things you no longer have actually were not that desirable in the first place.

Better weather beckons

You are beginning to feel — almost — like a normal human being again. You can see a life ahead of you; you can even make the odd choice about what you are doing. Time to address those vexed, post-separation questions that relate to loyalty, how to manage holidays and mutual friends.

Loyalty

This is one of many of those which-way-should-I-go moments. Loyalty should, as a matter of course, lie at the centre of a partnership where there are kids and, once dumped, I found it a particularly tricky one to call.

When I was in a partnership it always seemed pretty clear to me what constituted disloyal behaviour and what did not. A flirty local mum, for example, who boasted to near strangers that she often pretended to be asleep to avoid having to have sex with her husband, was, for my money, being disloyal to her partner. A close friend, however, who is permanently exhausted by her spouse's reluctance to help her domestically, and inveighs about him occasionally to people whom she knows well, does not seem to me to be behaving unacceptably disloyally.

One of the many difficulties you are perhaps grappling with now is the fact that your ex expects you to continue to be loyal to and about him even after he has been fantastically disloyal to you physically, emotionally and materially. Your default position is likely, initially anyway, to be a broadly loyal one, even if you are hysterical with angry jealousy, not just because of the kids but because you have always been loyal to him about the important things. Maybe you sense, at some level, the terrifying contents of the Pandora's Box that might writhe into view once you BOTH start being disloyal.

However, it is also a terrible strain continuing to be loyal when he has moved out and left a domestic train crash and distraught, damaged passengers in his wake. Surely the rules governing your relationship, if not the rules governing normal human 'intercourse', have changed slightly – bent if not buckled with the emergency services of friends, family, off licenses and chemists all standing by to help and unfortunately also to judge?

What to do? It is tough, this one it really is, and strikes a massive blow at one of the key principles of parenting – that you back each other up, reinforcing each other's positions and actions; otherwise it is deeply confusing for the children in your joint care. You do not want your kids either just to accept his behaviour because everything Daddy does must be right; or to despise and loathe him. Even I, as arguably the most ferocious and high-moral-groundish of critics of my ex, reckon that it would be unhelpful for his children to be encouraged to view their father as irredeemably base and disloyal!

Besides, if you were living happily with him and elected to reproduce with him, there must have been stuff that was good about him at the time. Is it possible that every single good quality that he appeared to possess has been swept away and expunged in the recent earthquake? It bloody well seems like it a lot of the time. Well, it did to me. The Bolter became shifty and almost blasé about his repeated lies. Everything was viewed through the distorting filter of his obsession with his new wife; and loyalty to the 'new' him in any shape or form became devilishly problematic for me.

I think, crudely, one possible solution here is effectively to split the difference on the loyalty front. You can certainly afford to be less loyal to your ex than you would be if you were still living together. He is now the father of your children as opposed to a member of your household and that is a massive shift which cannot help but be reflected eventually in your attitude to and perspective on him.

On the other hand, I do not think you can afford to be publicly critical of him. There are teachers, for example, who may have to deal with both of you, and it is awful for the kids if you cannot hold up some united front as their parents. By that I do not mean for one instant that you have to bite your lip when having coffee with one of your old friends but simply that sports day or the school play might not be the ideal forum for loudly detailing some of the more extreme outrages he has recently perpetrated on you or the children, tempting though it sometimes is, as he loafs around sanctimoniously soaking up praise for their recent xylophone solo or Mott and Bailey model. Did he buy, cook or eat endless eggs to liberate boxes for that particular project? I think not!

When parents whom I barely knew chatted amicably to my boys' father at various events as though he were a normal and decent member of the human race, my head used sometimes to buzz with rage. It struck me as deeply unfair and I felt morbidly self-conscious as we split up at the school gates and went our separate ways after functions while all the other parents strolled off amicably arm in arm.

The children, of course, have their own issues to negotiate. I remember finding my sons' loyalty heartbreaking when I overheard them boasting to friends about their dad's enormous new garden. It was in fact the heath over the road as they did not want to admit to anyone that his new place did not actually have a garden at all!

Endless ethical see-sawing probably awaits you on this one, along with the zillion other being-dumped ramifications currently causing you migraine levels of mental fatigue. I still find myself chopping and changing over which way to go on it. But I think the best rule of thumb is this: vent your frustration and misery when and where you can, but stop short of doing it in front of the children. Children are incredibly intuitive and often 'know' and understand far more than we realise. They know when their parents are unhappy.

My boys did not need to have spelt out for them the detail of their dad's betrayal. It was literally hanging in the ether – unbearably, burningly 'there'. Generally, you'd have to be superhuman to shield them from the unpleasant 'fact' of the manner of the split. But do do your level best not to bad-mouth your ex in front of them – ie, do what I can suggest now with the benefit of hindsight, not what I did then and now regret!

Holidays

Early on, post-dumpage, holidays are undoubtedly one of the times when you will feel at your most suicidally vulnerable. You feel crap and bereft as usual, but it is heightened by the fact that you and your children are supposed to be having a time of 'recreation and amusement'. You are not supposed to be thinking:

'Did I pack enough whisky and had I better hide the razor blades from myself?'

Because it is classed as a treat and more fun than term time and all of that, the pressure becomes unendurable and instead of feeling especially happy you feel especially sad.

Serious self-pity set in, I found, with sand. All around you there seem to be well-adjusted, picture-perfect nuclear families desporting themselves. Energetic dads build ambitious sandcastles while slim, smiley mums affectionately apply sun-cream to small wriggling shoulders and hand out sandwiches. Even families where one or both of the parents is away working a lot tend to spend the annual Summer holiday together and, as an onlooking dumped single mum, it really can seem intolerably painful.

One of my young sons used regularly to go and stand mournfully on the edges of these families on the beach, hoping, it seemed to me then, to catch some of their happiness, a desirable waft of daddishness perhaps. At those moments I remember feeling that I was the only person in the whole of Cornwall who had been inept enough to mislay their partner. The younger boy meanwhile would be informing anyone who would listen that his dad was actually in the helicopter buzzing overhead or behind those rocks at the end of the beach. Older children would shake their heads pityingly and I would want to kill everyone on the beach including myself and my children.

The trouble would begin before the holidays even started. I felt dreadfully hard done by having to wrestle with the choosing of the holiday, the booking of it, the paying for it, as well, of course, as the packing, the map reading, and shouting at children en route.

The children were too young at that stage to help. Unsettled by the suitcases and change in routine, they would panic and get under my feet. Even loading the car, if you live in a town, that is, becomes a major motion picture as you are worried about leaving the kids alone inside but clearly cannot leave the front door open as you rush back and forth in case they dart out onto the road. Strapping them into the car whilst you load around them is possibly the safest option but they are bound to need the loo before you leave, and they get fractious and it makes the journey much longer for them if you take as long to load the car as I seem to.

Trains are not necessarily preferable, though. I remember the impossibility of getting children, luggage and pushchair down a nasty double flight of stairs to the carpark in a suddenly deserted railway station. In the end, I had briefly to abandon the older child at the top and then the pushchair at the bottom while I flew between the two. And anyone who has had the misfortune to be in sole charge of two small children on an aeroplane, sitting between them obviously to minimise fights, and then tried to eat one of those meals, will understand the impossibility of avoiding catastrophic spillage as juice floods the roll, butter and pudding sections and hot coffee tips into your lap. Of course, parents are faced with this sort of dilemma all the time, but somehow as a single mum on holiday it can feel particularly excoriating.

So please do not get me wrong when I abjure you to look on the bright side and promise you the occasional ray of sunshine to brighten up the situation and warm you on your hols. I have been there. I have *so* been there. I have been unable to swim in the most friskily enticing sea as I have felt too sad, proud and anxious to ask strangers to keep an eye on my toddlers. I have sat in cottages for days and days with rain streaming down the windows and stir-crazy kids unable to contemplate another board game or galvanise them into a sopping blustery walk. The mantra 'you have got two healthy children and you are very lucky to be able to afford a holiday', chanted hysterically under my breath through gritted teeth has not, on those occasions, helped a jot. But that was all several years ago now and, while many upsetting memories will be burned in my mind for ever, things have slowly changed, the balance has at last started to tilt, as I see it anyway, in my favour.

Possibly things started to change for the better on my second proper summer holiday as a single mum, when I had a flash of inspiration and packed our sexy, irreverent, six-foot nanny into the car along with a few other key luxuries. She had a different view of the beach and a heartening knack of spotting the palest, crossest, most dysfunctional families toiling down the cliff path.

'*Look at her!*' she would shriek when a poor mum, laden like a pack horse in nasty sandals and an ugly floral skirt, was barely out of earshot. '*Poor cow. Did you see that?*'

Then she would repeat it for emphasis.

'*Did you see that?*'

'*What?*' I would ask nervously, realising that I had forgotten sun-cream and water for the second day running.

'"*Martyr*" *stamped across her forehead with a nasty, arrogant husband, carrying nothing and bossing the kids, who probably beats her up. As for those children, sullen, lardy and demanding. Nuclear families. No thanks!*'

And off she would skip in her skin-tight tankini,

boggling said dads with her show-stopping cleavage as she whooshed up the beach on my son's bodyboard. I would look at her amazed, thrilled and energised, and think:

'*Yes! For the purposes of this holiday, she is part of our family, not a dad exactly, but very bracing and in some respects rather better.*'

On the overcast early evening that we arrived, the children and I whizzed into the sea on principle and then struggled back shivering to our cottage which rather blissfully had its bath in the kitchen. Even more blissfully, aforementioned nanny had thoughtfully run me the hottest, bubbliest bath ever and made a couple of ice-cold gin and tonics. There I slumped in sensual heaven, banishing all memory of the early start and pig of a drive, and watching my brood lay into fish fingers that I had not even had to prepare. OK, that was a one-off, and she was not a lover with all the benefits that go with that role, but it was a cracking start to a holiday and definitely marked a mini turning-point in my slow emergence from all-engulfing depression.

There is nuclear and there is tragic, I realised, and then there is everything else in between and that is perhaps most dazzlingly clear to me on holiday. I cannot be nuclear, although I was for a bit and imagined that I always would be; and these days I refuse to be tragic. Immediately after the split it is impossible not to be anything other than deeply tragic. But one spring day you realise you might be wallowing in your tragedy, milking it just a bit, and that is when, almost without you realising it, things begin to change. When you really hit rock-bottom, there turns out to be only one way to go – up.

Since that second holiday we have tried every conceivable combination and permutation of friends, nannies, and cousins with great success and variety. For us now, no holiday is ever the same and that is what I mean about the exciting different choices ahead of you now – new forks in the road.

Once we had a suddenly single dad popping by with his daughter to camp in the garden for a couple of days. He was an exemplary holiday companion who bought lashings of wine that he stacked up in the kitchen with a grin on arrival, saying:

'*Always comes in handy.*'

He treated us to fish and chips in the harbour and otherwise just mucked in and wisely did not try to interfere with our routine. The nanny almost fancied him except that he wore rather large leather hats. You cannot have everything.

On another occasion, a friend dropped by for a couple of days with his wife, three sons and 70-year-old mum, which would have been absolutely unthinkable if my partner had still been in situ, and they were fantastic as well. The wife was merrily elbow-deep in the sink within minutes of her arrival, the gran tried bodyboarding for the first time in her life, told ghost stories round the bonfire in the evening and wisely stayed in bed reading Dostoevsky to avoid the morning breakfast and bathroom bottleneck. Their kids roared around with mine, the food was nicer than usual as they were better cooks than me – not difficult – and I had had so much generous hospitality at their hands post-dumpage that it was a relief to be able to pay them back a little, well sort of, with them doing most of the work!

So, if you find holidays daunting and you fear feeling exposed and sad, then try taking people with you or having the odd visitor for a sleep-over. That can give you a bit of structure, take you out of yourself; the kids can put welcoming flowers in jam jars and there will be other adults and children for your children to harass and hang out with as well as you.

Take enough sympathetic other people to disguise the gaping dad-shaped hole which is so debilitating in the early days after the split, although I would caution against too many visitors all at once. If there are lots of guests, it can easily become a mass catering nightmare, with wearisome financial issues bubbling under the surface. Ring the changes. The dynamic does not always work if people want different things out of holidays. Then again, were holidays with your partner ever totally tension-free? I think the trick might be to encourage short visits from people you like and feel safe with. Being locked by a panic last-minute decision into two weeks with a bossy self-righteous family, where you spend your life trying to read their shopping lists or committed to hearty expeditions with them that your kids do not want to go on, is clearly not an ideal solution.

There is one other distinct upside to going truly solo in the holiday department. Before we broke up I used to nip off without the kids occasionally for the odd weekend break with a girlfriend or on a lightning solo expedish to visit a sister in France, but it always felt like a special concession, borrowed time that I would have to pay back to my partner somehow. Even obligatory work trips fell into that category, absurd as that sounds, particularly as my then partner used to travel all the time and we both weirdly felt that that was his right. I knew this at the time to be deeply unsound as an imbalance but all I can say in my defence is that a lot of other women I know with kids in relationships feel the same way. When you are in a relationship and go away on work or a tiny break, you worry about the kids, feel stupidly grateful to your partner for caring for them; and, in the end, all of that emotional expenditure almost neutralises the boost of being out of the house and a supposedly free agent.

I remember, for instance, going off with four friends for a weekend to a beautiful place to celebrate my 40th birthday, just for a couple of nights without the children. One of them, a high-powered professional with three teenage children, nervously admitted that this was the first time, ever, that she had been away without her kids or husband since she had been married, apart from very occasional work trips. She did not feel able to achieve it for herself, could not really justify it. Not everyone is like that obviously, but these days I do utterly relish the fact that, as long as there is someone available to look after the kids and they are OK, no one is counting, and no one is exacting an emotional payback for my little tripettes, forays and excursions. Hooray. That is the paradox. You are notionally less flexible as there is only one of you, but you are also freer as there is no one else to convince that you need, have earned, deserve and, above all, want a jolly break away. Again!

Fairly soon after being dumped, I was given three months leave of absence from work. I realised that it was a pretty rare chance to go walking with a friend along the Italian coast but, fairly inevitably, her schedule did not fit with mine unless I missed the last day of term. The boys broke up at lunchtime and I had never before been able to take time off work to be there, coming as it did after a rash of sports days, school plays and with the summer holidays looming. This represented my one chance, I thought, to take receipt of those ghastly collapsing loo-roll models of the solar system and chat to other mums and give the form teacher the small pot plant she almost certainly didn't want.

What to do? I agonised, I debated, I bored everyone rigid and in the end went to Italy. At the beginning of the autumn term I remembered belatedly that I had never seen my son's school report. What had happened to it? Had he lost it, hidden it from me or binned it? On cross-questioning him ruthlessly, he swore blind that he had handed it to me on the last day of term.

'*I definitely remember, Mum. I gave it to you outside*

school on the day we broke up. I even remember where you were standing.'

I smiled and smiled for the rest of the day. Emotionally scarred by my passing up the opportunity to pick him up on his last day? I do not think so. In his mind I had been there anyway, tee hee, and the sunshine and sea and squid outside the school gates had been great, too.

Holidays are for treats and indulgences, I think, for kids as well as adults, and God, it can be so much easier when you only have yourself to negotiate with. You can allow your toddler to have chocolate biscuits for breakfast as you are enjoying your coffee in the sunshine and cannot be arsed to argue, ditto you can cave in over extra pocket money for the kids to buy tacky car-boot sale items without anyone criticising you. You really, really can let the day speak to you, and change your mind endlessly with no implications if you are the only adult. There is no:

'We really should have brought a picnic' / 'I knew the weather was going to turn' / 'I said he was too tired to enjoy it.'

It is true that there is no one to help you pack the bags, but there is no one either to insist on an educational visit to a historical site when the kids want to buy virulent slush puppies and see a rubbish summer film for the fifth day running.

I remember getting lost once with a bevy of single mums and getting back horribly late with whingey, starving children of all ages to an ill-equipped holiday cottage. Within seconds, it seemed, and no conferring, the younger ones were bathed, the table was laid, supper was cooked, wine and hot chocolate was poured and everyone had been utterly relaxed about the mechanics of achieving it.

We amused ourselves then by rewinding twenty minutes and pretending to be our exes shouting bossy and contradictory interventions regarding who should do what, that wet swimmers simply must be got out of the cars before anyone could sit down, carrots had to be chopped more finely for cooking, why was there no ice in the bloody fridge, the absolute necessity of making work-related mobile phone calls, and so on. It would have been a fraught nightmare, we all concluded, with loud recriminations, tantrums from the kids and the meal taking centuries to get on the table.

When I am on holiday these days, I am struck by how often I hear frazzled and defensive wives droning on embarrassedly:

'*Oh well, you see the thing is that Roland doesn't*

really like... the sun, the sea, cream teas, the other people on the camp site...'

And so on, and so on. How often, though, do you hear?

'Oh, Delilah doesn't like playing with the children on the beach so I do it all and then she can relax with a book, flirt with a lifeguard and generally do her own thing!'

Not enough. Not ever.

And what about when the children go off on holiday with your ex? Again, for a long long time, I found it hard to settle and enjoy those absences. The empty house, the quietness of the mornings would unsettle me, and I would feel anxious about them and hard done by. Eventually, though, I began to welcome the change in pace, revel in that head and house space and freedom to go away myself, stay out late and sleep in. These days I do find – at last – that it can be pretty heavenly to have irresponsible child-free segments from time to time. I think about my children a lot when they are away but I do not feel seriously bereft anymore.

Of course, the bickering over dates and competitiveness over giving them a good time still bubble up occasionally. It can be hard, particularly when there is a big financial discrepancy and the kids are being offered mega holiday treats by one partner, which on balance is usually the dad. Mums, though, can be better and more receptive to what their growing children need and want on holiday and that is about company, activities and no nagging, as much as it is about material resources.

Remember that you have only yourself and your kids to please, unless you choose to involve other people, whereas he almost certainly has his new girlfriend to accommodate and she may even have her own kids to soothe and enchant as well. Mixing all the kids together will undoubtedly prove unrelaxing, unless they all bond instantly which, although possible (and good on them if they manage it), is pretty unlikely.

So hang in there. I promise you that these days I feel only mounting excitement at the prospect of a 'family' holiday, with not even the tiniest smidgeon of sadness that there is only one parent aboard – me!

Friends
When I was first dumped, the fact that he was in a new life and in contact with anyone we had been friendly with, instead of being a leprous pariah in a social desert, was quite scalding enough in itself. I really

thought his sins made him unsuitable for inclusion in anything ever again. At the same time, though, there was something troubling about watching his oldest friends slagging him off and deserting him in droves. It was another variant of the ongoing loyalty dilemma.

The situation is further confused by the fact that, at first anyway, you want to keep tabs on him. You are in fact obsessed with it. You absolutely need to know that he is already fighting with his new floozy over maintenance, that he looks harassed and depressed and slightly uncared for and that he is missing his kids desperately. And his friends are one of the painfully few conduits available to you of establishing said. How many people do we know, including ourselves, who have asked in that thin tight pretending-not-to-care voice:

'So how did he look when you saw him at that party last week?' (What was he wearing, eating, doing?)

God you want to talk to his friends and God you do not – in case they like his new girlfriend – and God they do not want to talk to you if they can possibly avoid it, as you are boring and in a state and they are old friends, after all, and do in fact reckon that they owe him some allegiance, whatever he has done, in spite, of course, of feeling sorry for you... You have to be superhuman not to fall into the trap of pumping his mates for any information about him and then feeling hacked off if it is not what you actually want to hear, which it never is.

After a while, though, the correct turnings often seem to suggest themselves. Those friends of his, for example, who had always emphatically and historically been his, and who enthusiastically attended his, in my view, freakishly quick wedding or instantly invited him and his new wife round for celebratory meals, and so on, I just stopped seeing and being in touch with.

It was easier and cleaner, and in retrospect exactly the right course of action. The few genuinely mutual friends were a bit more problematic; but how many close friends does one actually need and have time to pay proper attention to anyway?

I have never been outstandingly good or bad at making or keeping friends but I cannot overstate the value to me of the newer friendships I made after I became a single mum. I have been supported, humoured, protected, rallied and admired in a way that has been fabulously restorative. Thank Christ for friends. Once you are alone for a bit, you are available and vulnerable in a way that you are not as a couple and there are nice aspects to that as well as the more obviously problematic ones. I assure you that sunshine and blue sky will break through more and more now as you motor along.

Friends get you through and women friends in particular. Let me trumpet loudly that friendship is one of the single most effective weapons in your emotional survival arsenal. I remember the intense gratitude I felt towards a mate who exulted in my young son managing to swim his first couple of strokes ever without armbands in a rock pool. The potential rushing sadness of:

'Oh God, yet another developmental milestone his dad has missed — I can't bear it.'

…was transformed, thanks to this girlfriend, into a how cool, what fun, isn't-he-ahead-of-himself shared sentiment which I still recall with a glow of pride!

I feel, which I know is rather fanciful, that a cat's cradle of e-mailage to and from female friends, usually working mums like me, some single and some not, prevents me on an almost daily basis from plunging into the abyss of self-pity which can unexpectedly open up under foot.

The subjects range merrily from troublesome teenager anecdotes through professional traumas to social gaffes, good fiction, bad news, any subject under the sun really, even the fact that another friend and I were too vain to buy large-size rubber gloves although medium were obviously too tight and kept splitting. This intimate warming skein of friendship streams across my computer screen sustaining me through everything and I value the contact more than I can easily convey.

Male friends for obvious reasons tend to be a more complicated kettle of custard. I find that I do enjoy a slightly different relationship as a single mum with the ones who are happily attached or who clearly have not got other agendas that I would say on balance is more fun than when I was part of a couple. It is hard precisely to define but I think having to embody many of the roles and qualities of mother and father, one is viewed as heroic and empowered by friends and therefore less hemmed into that 'wee wifey' box with regard to conversation and activities. People know I am raising the children pretty much unaided while attempting to earn a living and attend school functions and bla bla bla, and there is somehow an implicit acknowledgment of that, an ongoing comradely salute from bystanding men which is boosting.

The fact that you are no longer in a conventional

family – although the way the statistics seem to be going we may end up being the norm pretty soon – seems to free up the social structures around you just a bit. I quite often have just women to supper as it is fun and I have great women friends with lots in common and, with no men around, no one ends up hogging the conversation. Once you emerge blinking into the sunlight of your new journey you will certainly find different possibilities for friendships opening up if, of course, you are open to them. Take up previously unknown opportunities to see what works for you, heartens you, replenishes and sustains you. New friends are one of the many pleasing aspects in your new landscape.

And relations

Relatives on both sides are notoriously unpredictable when it comes to break-ups. With any luck your closest relatives should side with you and the mutual support should not wobble too catastrophically. It is worth saying, though, that even they can be shockingly tactless.

My elder sister knew someone who knew The Bolter's new squeeze and in fact was in the same book club as her. To my amazement my sister seemed to take pleasure in passing onto me how interesting and sensitive her friend found the new woman and how much she enjoyed their encounters. That to me was a shocking betrayal. I did not want to hear lies exactly, but I certainly didn't need my own sister to tell me how exceptional my nemesis was and with quite such relish.

My otherwise supportive brother told me, practically as my partner left, that my children would eventually have to meet and get on with their new stepsister and I should not try to impede that process. That idea, if logical, was also problematic for me to hear quite so soon from a close member of my own family. Which leads us neatly into...

Step Relationships

These 'new' relationships may endure and become significant, but my children will almost certainly never speak to, nor see their erstwhile stepmother and stepsister ever again. They passed through, as it were, but while passing were accorded absurdly high status in my children's lives. How can you un-become a mother or a sister?

It is an odd thought, the notion of people being parents and siblings and then suddenly not being any longer. How can you have two brothers just for a while?

It is a tricky area, this one of steps, and it is ticklish to discuss without indulging in hearty, agony-aunt-style generalisations. My kids used to ask me over and over again:

'Does our dad love her more than us?'
— meaning their stepsister, because his decision to live with her and not them seemed to suggest that he did. He, fairly unsurprisingly, refused to engage with that one and it was left to me to try to reassure them. You need to make sure that you do this, muttering whatever soothing platitudes you can:

'Daddy hasn't and will never choose anyone over you' (whatever you may think inside).

I am afraid that again it is best, if at all possible, to try and bite your lip, and encourage your children to embrace their new stepsiblings, however much that might rile you. I know it is far from easy and I certainly don't have an impeccable record on this one! In our case there was no long-term relationship forged because it was a genuinely difficult situation for them all, but I do know of friends whose family lives have been hugely enriched by the addition of stepsiblings.

And what of *his* relatives? This again can be a tough

one and I do accept that some grandmothers are so dottily devoted to their feckless unfaithful sons that it is almost impossible to maintain any sort of meaningful contact with them after the split.

If, though, post-crash, you do manage calmly to continue your relationships with grandparents and cousins on his side, it can be rewarding and make you feel pretty damn grown-up. It is usually us women who have put in most of the legwork on that front prior to the split anyway

The mother of my ex, not the easiest person initially, has got closer and closer to my children over the years which has been great, especially as my own mother is dead, making grandmothers thin on the ground. She lives abroad, and regularly sends us all in turn chatty letters and little advent packages and money and funny drawings. What a woman, we say!

As it happens, The Bolter's three sisters and their kids have always been sympathetic as well as good fun and stayed in touch and we would have been considerably impoverished if we had cut them off for being somehow guilty by association. They even come and spend chunks of the summer with us. I think cousins can be great as they are less intimate than siblings but often closer than friends. You should only chuck all that away if the price you are having to pay is too great. If, for example, his sister persists in telling you that all his other girlfriends have been more attractive and nicer than you, or his mum tells you repeatedly how well he looks these days and how much happier he seems to be since he left, give them a wide berth. You do not need that.

If you get pleasure and succour from his relatives, however, then you should stay in touch and feel deeply mature for so doing. It's a win-win choice, and about time too.

Respray and service

Things really are looking up. It is time to enjoy some treats,
plunging back into sex, shhh... and underwear as well as
home solutions.

Treats

Rewinding just slightly: in the immediate aftermath of the crash you needed to be spoilt and
you needed to be mended. You needed treats then
more than ever, and I do not think that this is a habit
that should necessarily be broken when you start to
feel better. Why not view it as a benefit that you carry
on into your jaunty new existence?

I am not talking about very expensive treats: mini-breaks in the Caribbean or Rolex watches, nice as they might be. You probably can't stretch to those just now anyway. I am thinking more of swanky bath stuff that smells orgasmic and is absolutely not to be left on the side of the bath to be used by kids, au pairs or visiting relatives – the kind with gorgeous packaging and a frosted glass bottle and a heavenly heavenly smell.

When you go out or flop into bed or whatever it is going to be that night – when you are feeling particularly post-dumped low – you can at least float about in a gloriously well-oiled and delicious cloud. Normally you would look longingly at this type of product in the shops around Christmas time but die rather than even think about buying it for yourself. In these circumstances, though, you must view it as essential and medicinal, and snap it off that shelf without compunction, for your own exclusive use.

As a mum with a partner and, possibly, a job and endless demands being made on you by everyone day in day out, you may not have been in the habit of spending money on yourself. Now is the time. It really is, and at any stage in your post-dumped journey when you feel especially dispirited. Get yourself some special treatish food that you really like, Belgian chocolate maybe or take-away sushi, delivered to the door when the kids are in bed. Yes, it is costly to indulge too often, but once in a while it's a must.

Perhaps your ex did not like Thai food; well, now you can hoover it up non-stop to make up for lost time. He certainly did not enjoy the spectacle of you curled up on the sofa with a hefty gin and tonic and no apparent supper plans, engrossed in a major phone call with a work colleague or your mum or whoever. Now that is absolutely a treat option when being semi-horizontal is all you feel up to and the kids are in bed and you do not feel that hungry and you cannot be arsed to tackle any of the million delayable chores that are tiresomely looming on the sidelines.

Sure, you have obligations to your kids, not least buying food, preparing said food, washing up, preparing more, washing up, remembering to buy more jaffa cakes and on and on. But when you are in that Groundhog Day of a supermarket situation, check out the grown-up delicacies sections, the easy-to-prepare really nice treats. Why not?

Listen to whatever music you feel like, loudly, and dance. Buy that country album that he would certainly have scoffed at and blast it through the house. The kids will be amused if nothing else. One of my abiding memories of that type of response was occasioned by the self-righteous 'We are getting married' letter which arrived a few months after my partner had left us. I was saved from meltdown by a Beautiful South track with the refrain 'Don't Marry her, Fuck me'. At that stage the kids, fortunately, were too young to hear and understand the words but they were undoubtedly heartened by the spectacle of me capering round the kitchen with them sing-shouting along. It made a welcome change for them after seeing me snivelling in the corner with dirty hair, ignoring their requests for entertainment or biscuits.

On the free treats front, there are a few that can be appealing and should not be turned down. Not least mates asking what they can do. In some cases it is simply a form of words meaning:

'I'm sorry for you and I do care, I really do.'

But any mates or relatives worth their salt, specially in the early stages, should be glad to help you out with the odd thing. One female colleague got her delightful hubby who was between film jobs to do a huge supermarket shop for me one day, which was wonderful. I felt really cherished and still remember it as one of the significant treats of that bleak first year.

Even when you start to feel better, support is still a boost so when someone offers, for heaven's sake, take them up on short stints of babysitting. However ghastly and difficult your kids have become, no one can really mind holding the fort for forty minutes while you storm round the park or sit in a café over a gooey cake with the paper, can they?

One thing I cannot recommend highly enough is going to the movies by yourself. It is great. There are no exhausting arguments about what to see; you can swing in feeling cool and independent, for the ads or not for the ads, and lose yourself in that technicolour world in the dark. You do have to be a bit wary of romantic films, for obvious reasons. I remember one Saturday night shortly before dumpage, when things were clearly not right, and my so-called partner was missing the other woman so desperately that he could not even be arsed to hide his yearning for her or try to talk to me, I left him with the kids in disgust and went off to see a black and white film called *Go Fish*. I had heard it was funny but also – critically – knew that it was a charmingly understated lesbian romance. At the time I was on such an emotional knife-edge that one single solitary celluloid image of heterosexual lurve or passion would quite possibly have caused me to hurl myself under the nearest tube train on the way home.

One of the definitions of the verb 'to treat' is '*to operate on a disease*' and we can safely say that not having had your hair decently cut for years counts as a disease which needs to be operated on. I am not advocating a misguided lunge for the peroxide bottle here. But it is undoubtedly true that a stylish well-judged haircut will make you look younger, more dynamic and better able to cope. And then, magically, you might actually find that you are... some of those things, for a bit anyway.

I know there is always that moment when they are brushing your hair in the nicely lit mirror and asking you what you want and you suddenly panic and think:

'Actually, I look OK and maybe this is a mistake.'

Trust me; the only major mistake at that stage would be to turn tail and flee sobbing out of the salon. Have that funky haircut, buy those expensive, soothing filling-out and filling-in products in designer packaging and skip out into the sunshine to a flurry of heartfelt compliments from colleagues, kids, friends and neighbours. Yeah!

My final observation on treats is that when people spoil you, have you round, look after you in some nice, thoughtful way, do not go into a paroxysm of guilt that you cannot pay them back easily. Try to relax, calmly accept their generosity and the fact that the rules have changed from when you were part of an apparently functioning couple. People want to help and know that it is tough for you and that is OK. One woman sent me a beautiful, expensive bouquet of flowers out of the blue as she thought I looked a bit down. It was gorgeous and unexpected and I certainly thanked her but I did not do anything in return as that was not the point.

Pamper and indulge yourself and allow other people to spoil you from time to time. In the fullness of time you will feel up to reciprocating in the right way – even if it is just being patient to another ranting, recently dumped mum, or taking her kids off her hands for a pizza.

Sex

Now that you are a freewheeling, perking-up single mum, speeding on down that freeway, this is one of the most festive of the potential free treats available to you in your new incarnation. Excited? Apprehensive? Smooching, dates, new relationships are certainly all out there now as a guilt-free option for you. Well, guilt-free as long as you do not start hitting on happily attached men, which is unlikely given what you have just endured.

When to embark, though, and how exactly to plunge?

At some level, of course – at the critical, vulnerable, just-having-been-ignominiously-dumped stage – one craves more than anything else affirmation of one's sexuality, attractiveness and femaleness generally. At the same time, in the first eighteen months or so after 'it' happens, you are almost uniquely ill-equipped to achieve any sort of remotely sensible new relationship at all. Not least because you have become SO FABULOUSLY BORING and self-obsessed and you CANNOT HELP IT. You burst into tears when something trivial and ridiculous takes you unawares. You might, of course, have got a bit fat, or horribly thin, with all the trauma, and you are not really used to anyone strange seeing you with no clothes on. All this added to your kids' savagely acute radar bleeping off if, in their new and intense vulnerability, they sense for one nano-second that you might feel interested in or affectionate towards anyone other than them.

The physical doing of it might be good for your skin, and as a means of counteracting your feelings of being a total failure on the attractiveness front. Then again, though, it is not great for one's self-esteem to feel indiscriminately desperate for a shag or even a snog just for the sake of getting back into any old vehicle after the crash. If you cannot decide which way to leap, just reassure yourself with the thought that it is impossibly hard to make the right call, in the early stages anyway, and you will almost certainly get it wrong.

If you are in the mood, you might manage a snigger over the breathtaking double standards that often seem to obtain around sex. Not least in your scrapped relationship with your ex, who, while reserving the right to do little else himself, will probably take a dim view of your own foundering attempts to re-form a bond with someone. It's a bit of a single-mum theme, this: he is apparently free to do as he will, but if you so much as dream about it he is likely to imply that you are an irresponsible slut and a bad mother to boot.

The Bolter was no exception to this. One day, striding into the kitchen, he angrily ripped a magazine centre-spread off the crowded noticeboard.

'I will not tolerate my kids looking at that!'

The picture in question was of an actor the kids had never met, whom I had never mentioned to them, whom I had slept with once. This incident had taken place shortly after my ex's own marriage to his new wife who, quite frankly, I did not want my kids looking at either. Annoyingly, I did not have the satisfying option of ripping her off the wall and scrunching her up in the bin so that my children were not exposed to her anymore!

A certain sports day at my kids' school relates in a different way to this unfair divide. A video producer father was sprauncing around in a leather jacket looking glossy and well sexed, having, as we all knew, recently found a much younger, sleeker mate than his gorgeous, if somewhat frazzled, wife could ever be. His ex, meanwhile, had gone very blonde and looked on the edge of a nervous breakdown but was trying to hold it together and share a picnic blanket and hoummous with him in public, for the sake of the children. That is how it is. Often. I am sorry but it is. I was that panicky, hoummous woman, symbolically if not actually, for several years and still do not feel I have quite become the self-satisfied, sleek, well-sexed-cat-got-the-cream to the degree that I would like.

It can be dangerous, however, to wait until you feel calm, collected and relatively sane to dip your toe back into that scary physical intimacy pond.

Have you heard the one about the devoted single

mum who slaved away trying to give her abandoned kids the best possible upbringing? Finally, after years of celibacy when her girls were in their early teens, she got it together with the decent unattached local vet who had looked after the family pets for ever. He was ideal and God knows she had hardly rushed into a new relationship speedily and ill-advisedly, thereby bruising her still traumatised daughters. The first night that the vet stayed over, he waited until the girls had gone to school before emerging. The single mum was faffing around with a spring in her step making toast, as the vet sat down cosily at the breakfast table and lifted the lid off the butter dish. On the butter one of the girls had written 'prostitute'. As a scenario, I do not regard this as ideal.

The trouble is that being dumped makes you feel you are rather crap at this whole game anyway. While your ex's sexual betrayal has left him feeling like that video producer, cockily energised and glowing, you are unlikely to feel at your most rampagingly desirable.

Was I really really bad at sex? – I found myself wondering a million times a day post-dumpage, having never given the matter much thought previously. To make things even worse, my ex had the bad taste to publish poems as he dumped me, alluding to his new-found joy in that department – which hardly enhanced my self-esteem on the sexual prowess front either.

But that is enough negativity as, currently, we are supposed to be at the stage of selecting goodies for ourselves in this new and more upbeat phase. If – and heaven knows it is by no means a shoo-in – one manages the odd bit of action, and by that I mean anything from a festive encounterette to a long and deeply satisfying relationship, there are some fabulous treats in store. Hooray. Being a dumped single mum does not necessarily mean solo occupancy of bed and sofa indefinitely.

Let us rhapsodise for a moment or two about kissing. Call me old-fashioned, but however good one's physical relationship of sixteen and a half years and two children is, however much respect and sex and playfulness one still had with each other before 'it' happened, did you ever grab each other after a day's work, in the kitchen when the kids were not looking and snog each other's lights out as though your life depended on it? In my case, er, not exactly.

Kissing is heaven. It can make you, me, us feel young and happy and desirable and I love it for that alone. I love it. It is probably documented in lots of places that women like it more than men. But when you embark on a new physical relationship, in my experience anyway, there is usually loads of great kissing and that feels fantastic. I remember one very long smooch in the bath with a new lover one afternoon that was not even a prelude to further action but simply a kiss for its own sake, zonkingly sensual and tender. It felt great, and I registered it at the time as a tiny moment to hang onto and remember as something that would not have happened in my old life.

Once, when we were going away without the kids, I met up with The Kisser in the pub. I remember thinking:

'But I am a mum in my forties and it is only five in the evening, for God's sake, and he is younger than me and I feel a bit self-conscious but actually this is bloody great!'

There was an attractive and sympathetic woman with a vast rucksack at the next table who grinned at me and clearly thought it was cool rather than tacky, which helped. And I relished that confusion, the derailment of my dyed-in-the-wool perceptions of myself. The whole affair was a blast. When people were pouring down his road one way in the morning, off to school and work, I was whizzing up it in the opposite direction for a lightning interlude with him before work. Just going against the flow of my normal routine like that was refreshing and felt wonderfully illicit. Even though the relationship only lasted eighteen months, I do not feel that I will ever forget certain aspects of it – certain compliments, and those kisses!

Sex is yet another area in which as a new single mum you must counsel yourself not to write yourself off, or play the martyr. Think to yourself:

'*Yes, I* do *deserve a bit of a life, and maybe some action now and then.*'

I remember being away on holiday one summer, and my boys going into a total bolsh that The Kisser in fact was coming to visit for a few days. I instantly felt nervously guilty and was on the verge of cancelling him when the right-on ex-nanny who was also staying intervened on my behalf:

'*You may not like him staying, but your mother and I will expect you to be polite to him in the way we'd expect you to be polite to any visitor.*'

Assorted mates in various houses nearby took an equally firm line when I turned up sobbing for wine and comfort the night before he arrived:

'*For God's sake, you're giving your kids a fantastic holiday, and it's only for a few days*' / '*It won't do them any harm at all*' / '*You deserve it!*' etc, etc.

My kids do not even remember The Kisser's visit anymore in the overall blurring of those endless lazy summers by the sea so they cannot have been that scarred by having briefly to share me with someone else.

Dumped mums generally feel fiercely protective of their kids, all too aware that they have gone through the mill over the whole bloody separation, and are therefore reluctant to ride roughshod over their needs.

But in some ways one's anxiety about even briefly unsettling the kids can be absurd when viewed from the perspective of their dad's utter lack of concern. If I am ever slightly attracted to anyone, I feel guilty and worried about my kids' stability before anything even happens. The Bolter, however, like a lot of men it seems to me, appears much more relaxed about such things. His new girlfriend was there in situ when the kids visited their father recently and her status only became clear when my younger son asked where she was going to sleep. There was no smidgeon of throat-clearing harrumphing or any, 'Lads… there is someone I want you to meet.'

One stunning, local, dumped mum, whose part-ner, incidentally, when they were still together hit on almost every other mum at nursery, acquired after a couple of false starts, a much younger, very sexy, very nice lover who soon more or less moved in with her. He was great, her boys liked him, and he even helped her realise her lifelong ambition of directing a short film. As far as we, the band of other single mums, could tell, everything in the garden was enviably tickety boo. After a year or so together, though, she gave him the boot. We were amazed. Why on earth? Had she gone off him? Had he behaved badly in some way? The answer was very simple. She had noticed that he had started saying a few minutes earlier each evening:

'Shouldn't the kids be thinking about going to bed?'

He didn't insist, he wasn't aggressive about it but it suddenly struck her that her kids were growing up and there was something not quite right about this. On the evening of the day she ended it with him, she snuggled up on the sofa with a video and a take-away and her boys, and felt traumatised but great at the same time.

I think this anecdote illuminates something – well everything, really – about single mums and how cool on the whole they are as a breed.

It can be stressful to find yourself in the position of having to make a choice between your happiness, on the one hand, and the kids' security and needs, on the other. If you are not careful you can get ripped apart with the anxiety of it all — trying to be fair to everyone except probably yourself. It is hard, I know, but you can actually do a bit of glass half-full positive-thinking around this. Instead of:

'*Oh God, I wish I could see him more; it's all so unfair.*' Try:

'*Tonight I will go out on a date and he can come back and stay the night, and that is my right and my treat. Tomorrow night I will stay in, hang out with the kids, my lover won't be around and that'll be cool as well.*'

There are guys, I'm sure, yes, there must be, who are right-on and sensitive and totally brilliant at living with other people's kids. If you have found one of those then good on you and enjoy it. In my experience, though, those kinds of men do not grow on trees. The nicest man I had an affair with, whom my kids did adore, and who loved housework and playing and spoilt us all rotten, in the end bored me and irked me because he was too nice. He did not have a life of his own and wanted ours. That was a real shame, especially as I have never subscribed to that deeply dubious, only-bastards-are-sexy theory.

So sex, yes please, on occasion, as it should be one

of the treats and compensations in your new life. It may lead to a longer relationship, it may be a short, joyful, energetic encounter or it may be somewhere in between the two, but, whatever it is, do not feel guilty, girls!

There is nothing wrong with having relationships that do not last for ever. Even if they are short-lived, they might well be restorative and good fun. You can dabble about merrily for a while once you have got your nerve back and discover aspects of yourself – pleasures, pursuits, whatever – that you had totally forgotten about. You have only got one life, after all, and, though you did not want your partner to leave, now that he has, you can, if you want to, try something new. From time to time. Why not indeed?

Leading neatly on from treats and sex is…

Ssssshh…

The unmentionable subject of… um, sex toys. There I have said it. Well, whispered it. Actually toys is rather an ambitious description, conjuring up whole hampers of stuff, eeek, whereas this is actually just the most cautious of venturings-in!

For a kick-off, then, can I please make it absolutely sanctimoniously clear that I would never in a million years have gone into a sex shop in my former life, and actually, come to think of it, still have not. In so far as I ever thought about such places I dismissed them as tawdry and frightening. As for sad, suburban, sex tupperware parties, or whatever they are, with loud, busty, in-your-face women harassing you, no thank you very much to any of that either!

Yes, I do know that attractively confident gaggles of young women in television dramas and shiny magazines extol and 'rabbit' on about this and that model, but I am too old, the wrong generation, a slightly repressed ageing mother, and I do not, have not, would not know how to... I am very much not an expert, then, on the sex-toy situation, and this book sadly therefore cannot offer road-testing, tables of effectiveness with stars, different brands, flavours, sizes and wattages. Yikes! I cannot quite believe that I am writing this.

Equally, though, I could not get to the end of this section without at least a passing nod to the subject – well, in fact, two subjects which I think have got relevance to your average single mum. Firstly, please don't dismiss the possibility of jolly motorised moments entirely and for ever, as I did. Some of the, eeek, vibrators are tiny, funny, seductively designed, brightly coloured and not in the least saddo-medical. Get the catalogue. Have a look. What have you got to lose?

And the second subject – roll of drums... – is underwear! Of course, undies are a minute, not to say teeny consideration within your cataclysmically upset apple-cart, but worth a paragraph or two, I feel, during this pit stop.

If in your past life, pre-smash-up, you always bought gorgeous expensive smalls and hand-soaked them painstakingly, then skip the next bit. You will not need it. If however, like me and ninety per cent of my girlfriends, you never quite got around to refocusing on underwear after becoming a mum then read on.

How much do I know about my girlfriends' undies? Enough, actually. I remember spotting one friend in a changing room sporting some gargantuan floral knickers with synthetic, sick-coloured lace edging and she caught me sniggering at them before we both screamed 'Mum!' in unison. Yes, they had been an Easter present from her mum a hundred years earlier and, absurdly robust, they were still hauled out by accident from the back of the drawer in extremis, having inexplicably survived house moves, fires and comprehensive underwear chuck-out sessions.

Another friend was equally mortified by a jiffy bag

that arrived one morning containing her clean, at least, but raggedy, dyed-in-the-wash grey bra and even more ancient faded pants sent on from her regular holiday cottage by the rollicking young phwoar of a laird.

At the other end of the spectrum, when I was lunching with a friend, a wisp of glorious crimson bra-strap briefly made itself known. This was a friend I had never had occasion to see in her underwear so I shrieked, for the entire restaurant to hear:

'God, Jo, what beautiful underwear; I can't believe it! How on earth do you find the time with two kids and four dogs and a demanding job with loads of travelling?'

She blushed prettily, the colour of her bra-strap in fact, and explained that all her underwear was so unacceptably drab and ancient that her husband had finally complained. He felt that she was letting the side down given they were ditching the children for an all-too-rare romantic weekend in Paris. As a result she had been shamed into buying new undergarments for practically the first time in a decade (so she turned out not to be an exception, after all).

In my early teens I remember ricocheting around in vibrantly coloured more or less disposal combos. There was a particularly striking bra and pants set featuring that Rolling Stones lips and tongue logo which my French cousins thought were the most vulgar items they had even been exposed to, only possessing matching white lace sets themselves. I remember galumphing bras with invasive seaming across the cups, not to mention my first ever monstrosity with massive painted hooks and clips that was inevitably way too big.

However, as cellulite sets in, and one is faced with one of the more depressing aftermaths of child bearing – elephantine, wholly undesigner, structurally complicated, so-called nursing bras, for example – some of us can lose heart. The attempts to feminise aforementioned with scraps of lace and scalloping are really off-putting.

At this point I can hear you thinking, or possibly even screeching at me out loud:

'For God's sake, don't you understand that I've lost him and he's gone off with someone who flaunted lacy black bras and wispy knickers and the last thing I want to do now is re-underwear myself. Aaaghgh!'

If that is what you are thinking, understandable as it is, let me urge you to hold onto your horses and your crossness for a second and reconsider. Nice underwear can make you feel stronger and more confident, and by that I sooo do not mean gross, inappropriate, mutton-dressed-as-thongs. Middle-aged mums in low-slung jeans revealing straining, plaited thongage as they stoop to lift up bags of shopping is not one of my favourite spectacles. Debacles in fact.

Do not emulate them whatever you do. What I mean are those benefits to be had – by you, for yourself – when you lash out on expensive, pleasing, flattering and gorgeous items. There are lots in this cate-gory which do prove to be machine-washable if you just ignore the washing instructions on the label, and if there is a disaster it is not the end of the world. Money is probably tight – it usually is in the circumstances in which you now find yourself – but I urge you to mark celestial new undies down as a necessity, priority, emergency ration, whatever, up there with alcohol, more alcohol, expensive chocolate, trashy magazines and babysitters.

I had undoubtedly got stuck in a rut on the underwear front. On reflection, it was worse than being stuck in a rut, as I remember feeling slightly complacent that I was not the kind of flibbertigibbet airhead who threw away money on flimsy, impractical gossamer nonsense. When my partner left though, bizarrely, one of the few positive moves I felt able to make pretty early on, was the squaring of my shoulders, the throwing back of my head and the marching into Rigby and Peller, Corsetières — or whatever they are called — by appointment to or for the Queen, Princesses and unroyalty like me at large.

I had expected to be greeted by a grey-haired, square-bosomed, no-nonsense matron of the kind you often get in the fitting section of department stores, who looks pityingly at your sagging undergarments, sighs ostentatiously and asks pityingly:

'Oh dear, let's try the Delia shall we? Any colour preference, dear?'

But no. To my excitement and surprise, at Rigby and Peller I got a softly spoken deeply pierced gothette. I had really gone in for the bras, but emerged with the most heavenly knickers as well. It was terrifyingly expensive, but all my purchases that day lasted and lasted and still look and feel terrific years later. I am sorry to bore on but, if I could have conceived of and designed pants for myself, these would have been they, with no nasty, scary high-legs or thong-like detail, but equally not that nasty, middle-aged shorts feeling. They — these pants — looked like creamy or black floaty cobwebs, but somehow held in your stomach and flattered your hips and minimised the bulges and best of all had a nice, calming cotton gusset. They were exactly the right image for me, neither scary bikini, nor old-lady nappy. And even now I hear celestial trumpets and brass bands playing in the distance when I slip, glide and ease them on. On the rare occasions when anyone sees them I feel damn superior. But equally when, for months on end, no one apart from me is exposed to them, the mere sensation of them manages to set me up on otherwise dull-as-dishwater days.

I remember, back when I bought it, I would put that underwear out on my bedroom chair and think, yup, it is for me and it is so scrumptious and I look good in it and actually it is not the end of the world if it frays and runs before anyone else gets the benefit of it because I feel better in meetings and in shops and when my boss patronises me as she usually does. Trala.

That is perhaps enough on pants and bras. I could go on for pages, but I think I have made the point. It is like that annoying ad *'Because you're worth it!'* and you are, actually, and dull old him isn't. Anymore.

Home
There are lots and lots of definitions for the single

word 'home' and some of them seem to resonate particularly with us dumpees. Home is described, among other things, as:

'*The fixed residence of a family or household / the place of one's dwelling or nurturing with its associations / a place to which one properly belongs, in which one's affections centre, or where one finds rest, refuge or satisfaction / the place in which one is free from attack, the goal...*'

Whether you have managed to cling onto your house or flat through the inevitable financial upheaval or been forced to sell up and move, these definitions help I think with what is important here, as you assess everything round you anew.

I liked my home and enjoyed living there and all of that, but had never given the concept of it much thought, to be honest, until The Bolter smashed his way out of it and off. Then I became increasingly aware that my house, home, protection from the scary outside world, was looming much larger than it had done previously. It had become my place of safety, my refuge; and it hit me fairly early on that I wanted, no needed, the house to be specially appealing, soothing and restorative for the children as well as for me.

Not long after the split my father bought us a vast and beautiful sofa to snuggle up on and hang out in. It was an impractical white but given the size I wanted it to be cheering and not an oppressive dark lump. I bought bright new mobiles and lampshades and jolly cheap curtains for the kids' bedroom that did not have all the associations of their father's past goodnights tangled unhelpfully up in them – bedtime being a classically miserable time in these situations. Little projects help as a positive distraction and can be a good way of gently starting to break with some of your joint past – when you are ready to.

We got a cheap fish tank and fish and put funny plastic toys in it and lights behind it and stuck on drawings of shipwrecks. It became a mad bathroom project and the kids gave all the fish silly names. Another good thing can be to move the furniture and pictures around – you are less likely to be tripped up every ten minutes by memories of him playing 'This is the way the lady rides' with the children when they were little in that chair on the landing.

When my friend's partner walked out on her during her father's funeral, which was peculiarly sensitive we all thought, she loathed the fact that he meticulously removed every last sock and paper clip that could ever have been said to have been his.

That is slightly unusual behaviour. Much more

normal seems to be the 'grab suitcase of immediate stuff and then take for ever to sort out and deal with the rest'. It is awkward for the dumpers coming back, of course, and perhaps there's a bit of them, too, that does not really want to admit to themselves that they have gone for ever, so they somehow feel more comfortable if their stuff is still cluttering up your bedside table. But that is the point: that damned bedside table. You should not have to wake up and instantly be faced with his clock radio and trip over his ugly summer sandals under the bed. It is upsetting, it is unfair and it is far from helpful the longer it goes on.

Make your bedroom appealing. At first bedtime is a woeful, smack-in-the-face reminder of one's unwelcome single status and a dire part of the day to be navigated. There is no one there to hug you and make plans with and rehash the kids' traumas in the playground with. Get some pretty pillows, appetising lightweight novels, a cosy hotwater bottle or maybe even a little telly. Put a tiny bunch of flowers or pot pourri on your dressing-table that smells nice. Invest in whatever small luxury you can think of just for you that might give you a little unexpected lift in the evening.

Bed is important, as it is where you feel worst

in the beginning and best as time progresses, either happily alone or mucking about with new lovers. I got a vast platform-bed built under the window in my tiny attic bedroom looking out over London. The bigness of it, the fact it could effortlessly absorb the children through the night with little disruption and we could all have breakfast in it like a vast ship on birthdays, felt absurdly daring and exciting, with no unhelpful dad associations. It has shelves and storage underneath and funny cubby-holes to put things in. I got pretty new lamps and lovely new sheets, none of which were designer or expensive but were still refreshingly novel and such a welcome change from the mismatched student bits and bobs which I had never quite dispensed with.

I also hung up big photos of my children that I could gaze at proudly from within my swanky new bed. They were still with me after all and were beautiful and part of him obviously, but it was not like looking at images of him. They were the nearest I could get, initially I suppose, to pictures of happiness from my recent past.

I put glass clipboards up in the hall with holiday shots, taken after the smash, of my children in the sea. Those pictures rallied me on those first, bleak, nothing-good-is-ever-going-to-happen-to-this-family-again winter mornings. Yes, I would think, dragging myself exhaustedly off to work having been trying to make sense of everything all night again, we did sort of limp through a summer holiday without him, well just about, and yes, the kids did manage some carefree frolicking moments in the sea at least. Those photos presented a front to the world, even if it at times it was a pretty fake one.

Stick some flowers in a jug on the kitchen table; they can be as cheap as you like, but a tiny thing like that often acts as a little flag waving cheerily at you out from the emotional wasteland of the household as a whole: Hello! I am pretty and bright even though the hoovering has not been done for days and the bin is overflowing with empty wine bottles. Thus, one tiny section of the kitchen where you sit and eat becomes just a little more appetising.

I remember, after The Bolter left, I felt neurotic about homework and bits of Action-Man flippers and other non-specific mess cluttering up the table incessantly. I craved a small island of calm and felt that flowers were a tiny promise of spring and hope in our wintry sadness. Flowers are not misguided, retail-therapy initiatives, after all, that you will instantly regret and have to shove into a cupboard and feel nauseously guilty about for ever more. The brilliant thing about flowers is that they always have built-in obsolescence. In fact, I get fed up with being given pot plants as they hang around sometimes still blooming, blooming, long after I have got bored with them.

At a time when you may well have terrifying money worries snapping at your ankles, you are probably thinking:

'*Yeah right, designer living when you're broke... these suggestions aren't remotely helpful.*'

But paint, for example, is pretty cheap, given the cost of everything else, and you and the kids can slap it on together. What I am describing is more symbolic anyway, and to do with swapping round stuff, and binning ancient junk and redundant toys. If you chuck things away, and generally clear the space, the chances are that you will feel a bit stronger overall.

Beware of embarking on overambitious refurbishment and culling projects, though, and then collapsing in a sobbing heap midway through. That can be counterproductive, as I discovered myself on more than one occasion!

Go to Argos or Ikea, if you can, and pick up cheap colourful items with your children for their rooms.

There are usually little desk or bedside lights for a couple of quid, funky waste-paper bins or grander, more expensive hanging seats, bean bags or big rugs. The kids will feel cheered – if their rooms feel like a reflection of their own somewhat ravaged identities, shiny things might help to rally them a bit, specially if there is no birthday or Christmas reason but just an out-of-the-blue:

'What would you like today to make your room feel nice? Let's go and find something now this minute!'

You will feel better, too, however down you really are in yourself, to see your children brighten briefly. Little visual changes can act as a tiny beacon flashing out optimistically towards a cheerier, happier future. And you can at least comfort yourself with the thought that you are now officially edging towards the final phase of your journey. You are launching your new existence and identity as an almost-jaunty single mum.

Picnics and party time

Hooray, you've arrived. The accident is firmly and squarely behind you now. Spread out the rug in the sunshine, unpack the glasses and break open the bubbly, as the savvy new you salutes the exciting new view unfolding ahead.

Identity

One of the biggest benefits to me of my crash, and of the subsequent journey I was forced to make, was the wonderful sensation of rediscovering and then revelling in my unadulterated self in a way that had not been so easy for me, for whatever reason, while I was in a long-term relationship.

Identity is defined as personality and individual existence, both of which you may feel that you mislaid in the immediate aftermath of being dumped. It is the other side of the loneliness coin once you feel strong enough to take a deep breath and flip it over.

There must be people, women even, in happy relationships who maintain their personalities intact while bringing up children and earning livings and supporting their partners and all of that. It can be damnably hard, though, for the you-ness of you not to get a bit rusty, a bit blurred at the edges. Did you find that you could easily stay true to yourself, without compromise? The boundaries of your identity that butt up against his can so easily get rucked up or frayed simply in the interests of getting on and getting through.

One of the keys to survival as a dumped single mum is remembering to savour possibilities and situations that could not have happened in your previous configuration. Now you are calmer again you can perhaps celebrate your new-found strength, achievements and redirected hopes. I was certainly slower to take decisions when I was not a single mum. I was more anxious to please people and much less clear about what I actually wanted to do with myself and the kids. These days, adjusting my social life and work around my growing children, I feel able to spin on a sixpence, accommodating any number of conflicting options.

I remember chatting to a funny woman in Aberdeen whose husband worked on the rigs, three weeks on and three weeks off. I think they had a pretty good relationship when he was at home. As soon as he left for his next stint, though, she would stuff all his things in the cupboard, expunging every trace of his presence and turn the bedroom into her dream-girly boudoir again. In that small sense, she had it both ways. She was a single person again in between bouts of being happily married which I thought was rather savvy and cool.

My house is now emphatically how I want it to be, with no dilution, no negotiation and no areas that I am not allowed to muck about with or change on pain of death. I feel comfortable in it, whereas a friend of mine is forever apologising for her husband's crude, bachelor-type cartoons in the hall, and another one who thrives on clutter is forever in conflict with her more minimalist partner. Of course, there have to be compromises in any relationship as you are not clones of each other; but, as a dumped single mum, you should occasionally remember to glory in the fizzing path you can blitz through your life when it is simply you, you, you, with regard to fine-tuning the things that suit you.

I can wear smart or hospital clothes at whim; eat breakfast twice; cancel grown-up dinner and wake the kids up to enjoy lightning in the middle of the night just because it feels right – and there is no one to point out that any of these decisions are ill-advised. Hurrah again for that. You can do all of these things when you have got a fellah, I am not denying that, but it does tend to be more difficult when there is more than just the one adult, you, to take into consideration. Before the split I often used to find that by the time I had fought my corner I had lost all impetus.

Of course, children need routines and boundaries and for one to be responsible. How heavenly it is, though, within a broad landscape of, say, no telly after a certain time on school nights, to flout that rule when there is something very good or totally silly on, and snuggle up with just your eldest. He may be a bit addled the next morning, but he will also be walking tall, complicit with you against the world of his younger siblings and that dull, fixed bedtime.

I remember one afternoon going with other local

mums to a kids' outdoor birthday party. We chatted and laughed, supportive mums as opposed to competitive dads – not that I am generalising here... – and opened the wine at teatime. Our kids ran around high on sugar and apparent lack of adult supervision and it got later and later. Yes, it was a school night, as it were, although none of the kids were old enough to be in the middle of exams or anything, but the mums were all too blissed out and woozy to bear to have to haul themselves upright and break that luxurious moment and round up the kids to go home.

As a friend and I finally dawdled off, children strung out along the pavement, she looked at her watch, focusing properly on the time for the first time in hours.

'*Christ!*' she said, panicking, '*Jim will be livid. Look at the time and it's school tomorrow.*'

And I thought:

'*Thank God, I have not got to go home to a row as there is only me and therefore only me who will pay the price of vile kids tomorrow, and today's washing up still not done, and we have all had a great time and I do not regret any of it. Not one jot.*'

I did concede, though, somewhat drunkenly to myself, that if my ex-partner had wandered home pissed this late with the boys on a night before school I would have been livid and quite within my rights to be so. It was a bit irresponsible, and all the mums kind of knew that, but only some of us had to suffer the wrath of partners, those that had them! There are always those maverick moments that you and your kids feel the need for, but gazooks, how much easier it is to enjoy them without guilt and confrontations if you are a single mum!

If you have been with someone long enough to have a child or children and still be together, it is probable that particular behaviour patterns will have started to solidify and this is not always helpful. One of you might be better at something and therefore habitually book the holidays, or make the children go to bed, or unblock the sink, or whatever it is.

Once you have been dumped, though, your whole identity gets manically rotovated whether you want it to be or not and what initially feels like savage dismemberment also yields up the odd benefit. When everything is up in the air refreshing alternatives sometimes come floating back down. You can change the rules, the routines and the holiday location with minimum stress or exertion. If you had allowed yourself to become the more indulgent parent in the partnership, you can now much more easily opt sometimes to be strict and vice versa. Your energy can go into making changes rather than being sapped by lengthy disagreements over whether things need to change at all and, if they do, how and when and for how long.

In my case, by the time The Bolter left I had become utterly crap at cooking. My mum had hated cooking and struggled with it all her life and I seemed to have caught cooking ineptitude and nerves from her. My partner liked cooking and was much better at it than me, not difficult, and I actually got worse, if such a thing could be possible, as a result of his supposedly affectionate mockery. It got to the stage that I could barely heat up baked beans for the children with any confidence.

Once he left, of course, I had to grasp that tepid potato, as there was no one else to do it and we could not live on picnics indefinitely. It was hard for me to gain any confidence around the kitchen and I still never attempt anything too tricky or time-consuming but I can at least now serve up half-decent food without having a nervous breakdown. More significantly, I have shed that nerve-racking feeling of inadequacy in a key area of life which is such a flipping relief in itself.

It can be liberating, too, I find suddenly to hold

forth on something in public without a partner exuding patronising vibes that you are bluffing and do not know what you are talking about, even if you do not. Everyone bluffs about most things anyway: politics, art, bringing up children. How can we possibly know it all? But is it not good fun sometimes just to have a view? This is a more complicated inhibitor than simply loud men oppressing their poor wee wifeys although that is how it sometimes appears. It relates to the building-up of perceptions, habits and fears over such a long time that you get to the point of no return: for when you do actually change your mindset or want to get better at something or stop doing something that you have always, always done, it seems almost impossible. You need to transform someone whom you totally trust's view of your capabilities, as well as your own, and that is doubly hard. By yourself or just with your kids, you can transform yourself over night. Well, maybe not quite, but it is certainly easier. I can be good as well as bad at cooking in one evening, for example, with no opprobrium. I find that sometimes I can do one child's maths homework but not the other's, as opposed to simply being blanket-irredeemably-crap at every branch of science.

My partner always scoffed at my hopes, one day,

to be a writer. After he had left he told me I had as much chance of earning a living as a writer as I had of winning a competition on a cereal packet. I did know that it was never his call, but in my defence I think most people find it hard to swim energetically against an oppressive critical, live-in male tide if they are unsure in the first place about their capabilities in a new area. I could not believe the thrill I experienced when a new boyfriend encouraged me to try writing. Stupid as it sounds, it simply had not occurred to me that a man I was close to might believe that I could achieve something new and high-risk like earning my living in a different way.

My journey towards a new identity really began with a physical journey. Shortly after The Bolter left, I had to drive my two small sons home from a summer holiday. This took more than eight hours and they fought non-stop and it was beltingly hot so we all had to keep drinking water, and then keep stopping to pee on the hardshoulder which was unbelievably danger-ous. Vast, chrome, container lorries whooshed past us, swaying and flashing their lights as I anxiously swerved out into the non-stop stream of motorway traffic for the millionth time. But we all got back in one piece and I felt empowered and exultant in a way I had never been before. I experienced that joy you see in a child when, after a major panic, they soar over a bar that they fear has been raised way beyond their capabilities.

Women all over the world are completing infinitely more difficult and dangerous journeys every day of the week, I know that, but for me the sweaty fear of embarking on that trip is still etched in my memory as a symbolic first step over a line in the sand. It was the moment when I had to start to facing up to some of the more demanding implications of the blow that fate had clobbered me with. And to my surprise some aspects of the process soon began to excite me. Reappraising my dusty previous identity, I chucked away the bits which had had me colluding in my ex-partner's views of my probable limitations and bolted in gleaming new replacements. And I discovered that this new combination of non-dependant me-ness, mum-ness, femaleness, fun-ness could lead to all sorts of replenishing impulses and adventures.

Festively, flexibly, socially well tuned

As a dumped mum you start off feeling horribly peeled and incomplete at each and every social event that you encounter and you cannot imagine that vulnerability ever evaporating; you have had your confidence smashed to smithereens and you panic that you have become socially invisible as a single woman of a certain age.

I was acutely self-conscious about my severedness to start with, and felt that I was conspicuously single at say, a new neighbour's Christmas drinks, visibly pouring blood from my having-been-dumped accident. Gradually, though, fighting my way back into the sunshine, things started to take on a different perspective. I swear you will eventually feel exultant about your reshaped social life. Kick off those clumpy old shoes and dance when you like, how you like, with whomever you like.

Whether you're going out more or staying in more than you did when you were in a relationship, it is totally your decision and all in your control and that can be pretty damn liberating and energising. Did your ex-partner's drinking mates, or business associates ever get you down? Who cares? You will never ever have to spend another moment in their company! You will not have to be patronised by his slim, stylish colleague who always makes you feel crap about your clothes. And you will never again be subjected to tiresome outings with the unspeakable wife of one of his oldest college chums.

In my experience, however well suited couples are, and, however much they elect to buy into their partner's relationships, there are almost always tensions round socialising. There are always those hideous moments when your face feels stiff from being bent into polite shapes all evening, when you are actually quite faint with irritation and fantasising hysterically about running home screaming, and slumping horizontally onto your sagging sofa in front of some particularly rubbish telly.

Bathed in your new-found confidence you can glory in the knowledge that there will be no harrumphing in the background if you accept a jolly-sounding invite. No sulky:

'*Do we really have to see them? But I've got a lot of work to finish...*'

You take that phone call and if you want to go you go, and if you don't you make up an elegant and convincing excuse. Even if you make the wrong call and go and don't enjoy it, you simply pretend the babysitter is having a fit and leave immediately with no naff whispering to your partner in corners because he does want to stay to the bitter end because he had promised to sort out some work experience for the hostess's delightful young niece or somesuch. You've had enough, fine, you simply flit airily out into the night ecstatic that you owe the babysitter less than you feared. Conversely, if you're having a great time you can stay and stay and dance and yack to everyone you want to, with no debilitating reproachful 'I'm-so-tired-and-bored-and-you-know-I've-got-that-fabulously-significant-meeting-at-dawn' acting from a disgruntled partner.

Now, even when attending the most intensely couplish of events, I usually feel fine and quite often slightly superior as I only have me to worry about. Am I enjoying myself? Am I keen to leave? Am I fit to drive myself home?

Socially speaking, you are pretty much over the hump and good company again. You can toast passing unattached males, hang out with female friends, couples, or your own kids, depending on your mood and go to most gatherings on your own terms. And that seems like a great deal.

Closure

One of the definitions of closure is 'the agreeing of terms'. At this stage in your journey, though, I think of it more as you agreeing terms with yourself and your new life than agreeing terms with your ex. A lot of the difficulties and pain are well behind you now and you can start to look ahead. What do you want to achieve? What do you look forward to and fantasise about these days? What will you and what will you not compromise on in the future?

All of that notwithstanding, can one ever really achieve total closure on something as major as being dumped by the father of your child or children? It is a tough one to call.

Even now from my new sunny vantage point, I admit shamefacedly that I still wish bad things on The Bolter and his now ex-wife from time to time, almost as a reflex, even though they themselves have been separated for a few years now. That is not particularly adult or resolved, is it? He appears to have a new girlfriend and, given that I no longer want to live with him, can I really have a legitimate beef about that? It is hard to say but I think perhaps I do have a few minor harrumphs about it just out of habit and perhaps also because she occupies a quasi-maternal position with regard to my children.

It may be that writing this book constitutes some kind of further closure or bits of closure. With each passing year you discover more things that traumatised you with regard to the split that you can now bear to contemplate or even laugh about, and perhaps that provides a long slow closure on it all. While writing, some of my past which I buried very deep has had to be exhumed and, while not hurting me with the savageness that it once did, it still holds memories of an agonising and very particular pain. I cannot envisage that hurt ever being wholly eradicated unless I lose my memory.

Without being unduly and unhelpfully pessimistic, I don't think closure can ever truly happen if you have had kids with someone that you really did imagine you would spend the rest of your life with and now are not. Something has been broken irredeemably, even if eventually you become happier and more fulfilled than you ever were with him. The memories and the bits of your children that remind you of your ex and the dealings you are still likely to have to have with him, prevent the gash healing over to the point of being invisible. How *can* there be complete closure? Even if, as the children get older, you never see him again, your intimate past together will always be part of your history, however much memories of that time fade.

And yet; and yet... as the horror and jealousy of the rupture recedes, and, as other things, nice things,

things that would not have happened if he had still been with you, slowly mount up between the moment of the split and now, you realise that the situation is nothing like bringing you to your knees anymore. It dawns on you that you have not thought about him or indeed 'it' for weeks on end. You buy new swimmers without even wondering if he would have liked or even noticed them and you start to take pleasure in taking important decisions with or for the kids without even consulting him as there is not the time and it does not seem necessary and you cannot be arsed to remind him anymore. Or is it rather that none of these things seem to matter – cause you pain – anymore?

You probably have some undumped friends in pretty crap relationships who lack the freedom and flexibility that you now enjoy. You may also have made some great new friends since being dumped. Whatever you have or have not achieved, the landscape around you has emphatically changed. You were a sad and sorry victim of his horrible behaviour for quite some time, but these days you look and live forward again and pretty merrily most of the time.

I read an article in the paper recently about a dumped mum whose ex was an academic. She scoured the internet for details of articles by him and about him for years and years after their acrimonious separation. Eventually the flat he had moved into with the 'other woman' came on the market as they were moving away or splitting up or somesuch. Anyway, there were comprehensive photographs of their erstwhile shagpad on the internet to encourage prospective buyers and the aforementioned dumpee could finally see this space, the thought of which had tormented her for so long, the bed they had done it on, even the special items and photographs of the grown-up kids that he had taken with him from their joint house and proudly displayed on the new mantle-piece. To her amazement what she had been dementedly trying to picture to herself was suddenly up there on the screen in front of her. Weirdly but also understandably, once that level of detail was available to her she felt she could finally stop looking. She had reached the end, exhausted by her quest, for what exactly?

For me that certainly seemed like some kind of symbolic closure and one which I imagine a lot of dumped women could relate to. It is almost the thought of the thing rather than the thing itself that is so hard to negotiate initially.

Yes, you are through the worst and your life has dramatically changed track in a way you probably never ever imagined when you got pregnant and had children. But, hey, it happened, and life is going on around you. You coped although you thought at the time you would never be able to negotiate the trauma, and you no longer feel tragic or embarrassed by your single mum status and neither, it appears, do your children. And, as a result you've achieved a freedom of sorts – there are so many pluses about your new situation. Your life is your affair now. You are in charge.

So let us raise a glass to us, the initially devastated and confused but latterly supercool sorted-out band of single mums who march on through, who get there and who achieve partial closure, bits of closure, whatever-kind-of-closure-you-can-manage-to-achieve closure. To us! To new attachments! But, above all, to a rewarding, unpredictable and exciting future... to the road ahead!

Dos and Don'ts
in THE IMMEDIATE
AFTERMATH

(I may sound fierce but, with the benefit of
hindsight, I do SO know what I'm talking
about here...)

Dos...

DO send him copies of their school reports
detailing how their academic performance has
suddenly plummeted.

DO drop the vaguest whisper of a possibility
of a new job in Australia.

DO accidentally kick nails and shards of glass
under the tyres of his parked car.

DO buy a goldfish for the kids or a new lamp-
shade or a boisterous bunch of flowers.

DO go for long walks with sympathetic
companions

DO listen to Mozart, Rossini, Vivaldi, and in
particular Laura Chantrell's 'No no no I'm
not the tremblin' kind'. Laura, if the colour
supplements are to be believed, is a shit-hot

stockbroker or city trader or somesuch
in New York City as well as donning
her rhinestones when she has a mo'
and is therefore a heartening role
model.

DO fantasise about murder, torture and
the major public humiliation of certain
parties.

DO customise a dartboard with drawings
or photographs.

DO stand very close to it while you're
taking aim. (DO NOT get it out until the
kids are in bed.)

DO throw away or hide all existing
fragments of his handwriting. An ex-
beloved's handwriting can, oddly, seem
more insidiously emotive and upsetting
than actual in-your-face photographs of
his face.

DO listen to any music at all that you liked
and he hated even if it's loudly.

DO sign him up to bake cakes for the

school fair and volunteer him to run that particular stall.

DO tell the kids you are sure they can muck about with his laptop when they're round at his and he's in the shower.

DO insist he attends every single parents' evening, sports day, gruesome school fund-raising quiz night and naff school play as he now DEFINITELY owes it to his kids.

Don'ts...

It won't make you feel better. You'll feel mud-dled and sad and angry and resent the petrol you've wasted driving round and round the block waiting for them to come back from work.

DO NOT, while you're in their vicinity – which you shouldn't be if you've got any sense, but temporarily you haven't got any... sense, that is, and I do so understand – try to peek through the blinds of 'their' new abode for clues, pounce on their neighbours with ridiculous inquiries or go through their garbage, to discover more about his new life style, however tempting it is.

Above all, DO NOT park or lurk behind a lamp post outside his house and spy on him as it will undoubtedly make you feel much, much worse. (If when mistakenly indulging in any of the forbidden activities above, you do see him – and, even, horror nightmare, heaven forbid, her WITH him – I absolutely guarantee that you will feel nauseous, miserable, inadequate and horribly tantalised by that absurdly expensive-looking carrier bag he is merrily swinging. You can't follow them inside and rip it open in order to discover whether it is something delicious to eat, or a cashmere sweater he has bought her that he can't afford and she doesn't need. I promise you that that little glimpse of them happily holding hands having purchased something glamorous but unidentifiable will undoubtedly dement you for days. On the other hand, if you don't see them, you will feel desolate, disappointed and angry with yourself for having lost an entire evening unproductively to them again!)

DO NOT throw your wedding and

engagement rings into a passing garbage
truck. If, you feel sick at the sight of them
and what they no longer represent, which
is fair enough, at least sell them or put
them away for your kids.

DO NOT go for a bad home peroxide job
that turns your hair purple.

DO NOT start borrowing and wearing your
teenagers' clothes.

Absolutely DO NOT confront him in his work
place.

DO NOT tell people you have only just
met that he still loves you really and will
be coming back shortly.

DO NOT go back to restaurants that you and
he favoured for special occasions.

DO NOT necessarily jump into bed with the
first man who asks you.

DO NOT get a shouty tattoo – laser removal
is very expensive.
DO NOT throw away all the Valentine cards

and funny little notes he has given you over the years. Just bury them deep in the attic for the foreseeable future. Then, if you still want to burn them, you can.

DO NOT change your children's surname by deed poll. Yet.

DO NOT attempt elaborate and ambitious dinner parties – either as a host or guest.

DO NOT attend any function involving karaoke.

DO NOT if you can possibly avoid it attend any weddings or christenings.

(But DO attend as many funerals as you can.)

DO NOT buy the kids a dog, a pony or a guinea pig.

DO NOT move to the country.

DO NOT accept a web cam for your computer so he can 'see' his children.

DO NOT commit to an allotment.

DO NOT go on holiday by yourself.

Above all, DO NOT get pregnant.

DO NOT throw things at him, her or anyone else in public.

DO NOT decide that this is emphatically the moment to experiment with non-prescription drugs for the first time. (Even though you have heard that amyl nitrate makes you giggle, which it does, uncontrollably.)

DO NOT listen to Wagner or Mahler or Leonard Cohen and, most importantly, DO NOT listen to Norah Jones. (Don't know why I didn't come….!!!)

DO NOT invite him over for a supposedly jolly Sunday lunch. The anticipation will stress you out all week, the food won't work and the whole thing will almost certainly collapse in a horrorfest of screaming recrimination.

Dos and Don'ts when you're feeling a bit stronger

Dos...

DO give him a reasonable ultimatum with regard to his removing all his stuff, including all that heavy hard-to-store DIY carpentry stuff in the garage i.e by the weekend after next as opposed to in the next ten minutes.

DO threaten to give everything away if he does not hit the deadline.

And DO resist any urge to feel sorry for him and extend the deadline into the middle of next year.

DO cautiously extend your repertoire and try out things you've always fancied but never got around to in the past, or he has dissuaded you from trying as he feels threatened or hasn't wanted to babysit! Eg. joining a book group, going skating, going to wine tastings.

DO ask him to talk the kids through marriage as a concept as you are finding it rather tricky.

DO go away without the kids, for however short a time!

DO have swimming or piano lessons if you have always wanted to.

DO ask him which charities he gives to regularly and why as it is very important that his somewhat depressed children focus from time to time on people less fortunate than themselves.

DO make new friends and arrange undemanding dates with mates.

DO take the initiative to go to exhibitions or matinees by yourself if there's something you fancy (but…DO NOT go the movies by yourself on a Saturday night!)

DO make it clear that your ex is to take on some of the duller child-related tasks such as those endless bloody orthodontic appointments in the middle of a school and working day and the buying of school uniform on that Saturday morning before school starts when the rest of the world has suddenly remembered that they also suddenly need grey trousers and nasty white shirts.

DO ask him in the strictest confidence how he will handle it if his son is gay.

DO ask him again in the strictest confidence to give some thought to what age he feels it might be appropriate for his pre-pubescent daughter to go on the pill.

DO ask his male colleagues, close friends and relatives with whom you are on decent terms, more in sorrow than in anger natch, if they would mind terribly being a positive male role model occasionally; kicking a ball about with your son, taking him to the odd rugby match. Whatever…

DO insist that he supervises the buying of presents and writing of thankyou letters to those of his relatives that you don't really like.

DO tell him how nice and generous all his friends and relatives are being to you and the children even if they're not.

DO drop subtle hints about the

hordes of new men in your life.

DO fantasise about his devastation at your own funeral when you have taken your own life, or died in a tragic accident and the children elect to go into care rather than moving in with him and his new partner.

Don'ts...

DO NOT feel embarrassed about buying condoms.

DO NOT feel guilty about refusing to change access arrangements at the last minute to suit him and her if it makes things difficult for you.

DO NOT get drunk every night.

DO NOT feel you have to be discreet about new men in your life for fear of hurting your ex's feelings.

DO NOT feel that you have to pretend to be fine all the time now as it is almost a year since he left.

DO NOT take up the violin.

DO NOT invite him to your wedding.

DO NOT go to his wedding.

DO NOT invite him to come swimming with you and the kids.

DO NOT involve him in Mother's Day.

DO NOT fantasise that he will visit you in hospital when you are having a minor some-what ignominious operation and even just possibly see the error of his ways…

In case of difficulty in purchasing any Short Books
title through normal channels, please contact
BOOKPOST Tel: 01624 836000
Fax: 01624 837033
email: bookshop@enterprise.net
www.bookpost.co.uk
Please quote ref. 'Short Books'

Caroline Oulton has worked in television
drama for the last twenty years. She lives in
London with her two teenage sons
and four-year-old daughter. Dumped! is
her first book